Making Sense

A Guide to Sensory Issues

Rachel S. Schneider, M.A., MHC

Making Sense: A Guide to Sensory Issues

All marketing and publishing rights guaranteed to and reserved by:

721 W Abram St, Arlington, Texas 76013

Toll-free: 800-489-0727

Local: 817-277-0727

Fax: 817-277-2270

E-mail: info@sensoryworld.com

Web: www.sensoryworld.com

Cover design by Joshua M. Erich

Interior design, John Yacio III

Illustrations by Kelly Dillon

Printed in the United States of America.

ISBN: 978-1935567561

To Sparky, my human fidget and beloved handler
To the "Unit," the best and most loving cheer squad a girl could have
To Dan Travis for pulling me to safety

And especially ...

To sensory superheroes everywhere, I hear you, because I am you

Contents

Foreword

by Dr. Sharon Heller

According to the media, psychologists, psychiatrists, physicians and most everyone else, Sensory Processing Disorder (SPD), a condition in which you misperceive and misinterpret sensory input, skewing how you respond to it, is a struggle faced only by special needs children and especially those on the autistic spectrum.

This is a misconception. SPD exists in a good chunk of the population, most of whom have likely never heard of it or gotten diagnosed as having it. Basically, if some sensations drive you batty, if you have two left feet, if the thought of exercise makes you cringe, if bright lights and loud sounds upset you, if you don't know right from left, if you get dizzy easily or get motion sick, if everything seems an effort, if you can't get from your house to the supermarket without a GPS, YOU likely have Sensory Processing Disorder.

In other words, it's quite common. Why is it touted as an exclusive problem among special needs children? Because this population generally gets diagnosed when they enter school, as it often interferes with normal functioning in a typical classroom. In neurotypicals, sensory input tends to be less debilitating, and people adjust and compensate. If you hate noise and bright lights, you avoid working in an office. If you are clumsy, you don't become a ballroom dancer. If you get dizzy easily, you don't go mountain climbing for your vacation. People avoid diagnosis by compensating.

Many people, though, ARE quite crippled by SPD. But since they function in the world, they get diagnosed instead with anxiety, panic, OCD, depression, substance abuse, eating disorders, and so on.

Rachel S. Schneider is one such person. She and her doctors assumed that her tendency to become easily overwhelmed was related to anxiety and resulted in panic attacks. When she finally found out about SPD, a light bulb went off in her head, and she pulled all her resources and became a spokesperson and advocate for SPD. A fully functioning, happily married, joyful, and loved person, she is in essence the adult poster child for SPD within a neurotypical population.

In this book, Rachel deftly guides the reader through a basic, SPD 101 course—what it is, how it affects your life, and ways to quiet its impact, all the while infusing it with a plethora of personal stories in her humorous, articulate, witty, and self-effacing style. The result is a book that not only informs but also is a fun read.

Sharon Heller, PhD, is the author of Too Loud, Too Bright, Too Fast, Too Tight: What to Do if You Are Sensory Defensive in an Overstimulating World *and* Uptight & Off Center: How Sensory Processing Disorder Throws Adults Off Balance & How to Create Stability.

Don't believe what your eyes are telling you. All they show is limitation. Look with your understanding. Find out what you already know and you will see the way to fly.

—Richard Bach, *Jonathan Livingston Seagull*

Chapter 1

A Quick Confession

Of all the sentences I could write to start this book, I think that this is the most powerful:

My name is Rachel and I have Sensory Processing Disorder (SPD), a neurological condition that impacts the way I process information gleaned from the senses.

On the surface, this statement seems simple enough. After all, I am named *Rachel Simone* after my spitfire great-grandmother and my soulful grandfather. I have always had sensory issues, long before I learned the terminology to explain why I was so sensitive and rigid with my particular needs. But the journey leading to my ability to write each character is

Meet your GUIDE ~RACHEL~

full of stories you might never hear: the complicated subtext of what it really means to have unidentified sensory differences in a world designed for most people, just not for me. This sentence is the voluntary raising of a hand and the wax-sealed invitation for criticism. It is the willing exposure of the most internal self and the first gasp of air after a lungful of water. It is both the most liberating phrase and the weightiest compilation of seemingly benign words, but from the first second I uttered it, I've never stopped repeating it to anyone who will listen. There's a certain kind of delicious freedom in the truth—especially the type of elusive truth that seems beyond your grasp, unwilling to be caught like a flitting minnow until, finally, in a single swoop through the stream, you capture it between your wet, wrinkled fingers.

Growing up, I always felt just shy of "normal," whatever that means. The people who knew me called me many things: "sensitive," "particular," "needy," "intuitive," a "homebody." I was outgoing, warm, and bubbly—a force of energy and empathy—until I crashed into a heap of tears, heaving cries that cleared as quickly as they began. I had strong, inflexible preferences. When things bothered me, they *really* bothered me—like the random popping of balloons and the feel of cream cheese across my tongue.

I actively sought repetition, routine, and predictability. I incessantly rubbed my face and arms against my grandma's mink coats and my fingertips against my stuffed lion's velvet-covered nose. I secretly chewed my cheeks, turning the flesh tender and distended. I was always covered with bruises, unsure of their origins aside from the general sense that I had walked into something again. I wore nightshirts to shreds, unwilling to part with the soft material made threadbare by years of use. And yes, let's talk about sleep—I typically slept with my body pressed against a wall, clearly seeking proprioceptive input in the days when this terminology wasn't even a twinkle in the proverbial eye of my dictionary.

Adults and teens diagnosed with sensory processing issues later in life always describe their childhood with a similar jumble of words, raking through the debris of their past for a single nugget of clarity. *Here,* they try to say, offering up armfuls of unrelated and inexplicable memories, *don't you see my sensory past taking shape in the rubble? Could I have known this information about myself sooner if someone had told me to look?* I find that I am doing the same here for you, bending and pointing at shards, attempting to assemble them into something that resembles proof. The bits and pieces, the particularities and the behaviors, seem unrelated at first glance but make sense when considered in the context of SPD.

The problem was I didn't have any sensory framework to turn to when I grew up in the 1980s and 1990s. The related words we have today were never a part of our vocabulary, even with the incredible work of occupational therapist and developmental psychologist Dr. A. Jean Ayres, whose ideas in the 1960s formed the pivotal structure for the ultimate understanding of sensory issues. I've met a few lucky sensory adults in my travels who were actually diagnosed in childhood at the same time I was growing up. While they were being evaluated, I was oblivious to the insidious root of my concerns. Sprawled out, supine across my bedroom floor, deeply involved in the latest episode of Eureka's Castle and holding my breath for the next family outing, I didn't realize just what I was missing. Sometimes I wonder if things would have been different if I had been able to describe the source of my discomfort or if I had realized that not all people felt the way I felt in my body.

As kids, we assume that all family units are like ours. We also rarely think that we're experiencing the world any differently from others because it's the only world that we know. It's this *egocentrism* that Swiss psychologist Jean Piaget referred to in his theory of development. If we think that people see, hear, feel, and encounter the same exact things as we do, we may not realize that our unique, problematic experiences are worth mentioning. I didn't know to point out the feelings associated with my experiences, because I assumed that they were typical. At a time when parents, teachers and clinicians were either less well versed in these issues or not at all, these figures in my life didn't notice the trends and patterns in my behaviors and sensitivities either. With no external identification and the inability to identify and verbalize the feelings and experiences that kept me in a loop of exposure to input, intense engagement and energy, and finally disconnection and bone-weariness, nothing improved.

During adolescence, a host of new milestones, like puberty and responsibilities changed the course of my life. I began having episodes of uncomfortable detachment in the face of unusual or intense auditory and visual experiences—but again, I didn't know how to view things through this particular filter. All I knew was that, when I was learning how to sing in Hebrew for my bat mitzvah at age 13, the sound of my instructor's deep, woody voice would somehow get stuck somewhere under my skin, causing my palms to sweat, my flesh to crawl, and my eyes—and body as a whole—to lose their tenuous connection to that exact second in time. It was as if I was feeling everything at once, noticing even the tiniest of details of voice and light and situation simultaneously.

The entire universe was vying for my attention, and everything was jumbled. When I couldn't hear sound, it was as if my eyes made an attempt to take in the information instead, and when I couldn't see the whole of objects, just their parts, it was as if my ears were trying to listen to the sights. Then, all of the information collided in an invisible, internal explosion. It was in this moment that I stopped being able to connect to the outside world. Unplugged and severed from my physical body, my motions became haphazard and jerky. Objects and sounds lost their meaning, and although I could tell you who I was, where I was, and the innermost details of my life, looking and listening became so painful, they were nearly impossible. Floating, detached from my body's physical presence, and unable to unravel the tangle of senses and information, I fought the urge to search for a nonexistent zipper on my back and unzip my skin.

It is an especially frightening experience to feel present in one moment and then trapped underneath a barrage of confusion in the next moment, somehow still a being in a body, but negated enough to feel like the body is a fortress and the being is a prisoner. Many people describe these sensations as a calm, protective relief, but for me it was painful, unexpected, and forceful. I could not escape the strange sensations when they washed over me and would be forced to stay stuck until a quiet, dark space allowed me to reconnect with my—now taxed—senses. These unpleasant events were a hallmark of my teenage years. Unaware of what triggered such an uncomfortable and unusual reaction, I began fearing their arrival. I started mentally tagging the places and people in my life when they corresponded to one of these episodes and avoiding them at all costs. I'd whittled my life down significantly before I was sent to a psychologist and received the diagnosis of Panic Disorder, an anxiety disorder characterized by acute and disabling panic attacks.

At this point in my story, I always take a quick break to regroup. The meaning behind a psychological diagnosis is a weighty one. It says that the experiences that we're having, as vivid and valid as they are, ultimately live somewhere between our thoughts and our chemical makeup. By working in psychotherapy to shift our approach to the world—our perspective, our understanding of the self, our willingness to accept imperfection—and tweaking our body's chemistry through medication when psychotherapy needs a boost, we can let many of these feelings go and live happier lives.

As a trained mental health counselor, I am absolutely in agreement with these statements. The problem for me was that the core of my battle was never psychologically oriented, but again, I didn't know this at the time and wouldn't know it for years. It's only been since the groundbreaking studies done in 2013 and 2014 by my friend Dr. Elysa Marco and the talented team at UCSF Benioff Children's Hospital San Francisco that we know that sensory processing issues have a physical structure. In a series of colorful scans, you can see with your own two eyes the difference in a brain with sensory issues and a brain without. (More on this in Chapter 4!) It is a very real, very moving sight to see after years of being completely in the dark. These scans prove that my sensory experiences, from my "sensitive" childhood to my overwhelming episodes, have a physiological, concrete origin. My sensory experiences are not a series of complex but mutable thoughts that I can work to wipe out from my consciousness, or a difference in chemistry that can be alleviated through medication. They're simply the result of how my brain is built.

Phew. Can you sense the relief? This is a crucial piece of information to have—a very forward-thinking, realistic nugget—so tuck it into your back pocket, because you'll need it as we explore sensory issues in this book. We are sometimes too quick to label the things that we don't understand in order to find some relief for ourselves and for others. For a decade and a half, I was told that my experiences (again as real for me as they were, that was never in question) could dissipate or at least diminish with the right combination of psychotherapeutic techniques and medicine. I was reminded again and again that, although I was experiencing my world in an uncomfortable and unusual fashion, I had the power to undo or reduce these symptoms and ultimately control and alter my physical experiences in the world. To some degree, this is true. I believe that, as an adult with sensory issues, I can change the way I approach my struggles. I can choose to see difficulties as praiseworthy challenges to overcome and envision myself as a strong, capable person. I can stay calm in the face of sensory overload. I can accept myself as a person with sensory issues and not fight their presence. However, my physical symptoms exist whether I un-think them or not. It's like telling someone with any other neurological condition—like multiple sclerosis or epilepsy—that their symptoms exist in their thoughts and chemical makeup: it's just not true.

That's not to say there are no psychological concerns. In my case and the cases of numerous adults and teens with sensory issues, there is absolutely a psychological component too, especially when we go decades without proper diagnosis and identification and are forced to make sense of nonsense. I clearly feared these attacks, these seemingly random, overwhelming episodes, because I didn't understand them, and I actively sought to control their arrival. To be honest, I'm anxious about most things in my life in a similar way, a diagnosis classified as "generalized anxiety." The day my diagnosis changed from Panic Disorder to Generalized Anxiety Disorder was one of the best days of my life. It was sometime after 2010, once I started seeing an occupational therapist—a suggestion from my truly talented, forward-thinking psychologist, a woman with a background in both psychology and neurology. When I asked about my episodes, those moments in time when I lost my connection to the world that I had learned to call "panic attacks," my psychologist said that they never were panic attacks. In fact, I never actually had Panic Disorder. It was the first time that someone validated something so crucial about my sensory self.

Since 2010, my relationship with my sensory issues has morphed and grown. Immediately after my evaluation, I was relieved that my 27-year-struggle was over. As tough as it was to know I'd always live in this sensory body, at least my challenges were recognized, and at least there were ways to make significant improvements. Before 2010, I never felt like anyone believed me when I explained how I was feeling or what I was experiencing. Suddenly, not only did people believe me, they applauded me for my diligence and strength in the face of isolating and difficult circumstances.

Even though I had finally reached the external acceptance and understanding I'd been looking for, I spent the first few years of my post-evaluation life feeling very angry and confused. I kept asking big, unanswerable questions to no one in particular, like, "How had I made it this long without understanding the most critical aspects of myself?" and "How had my SPD gone undetected?" I hunted down and voraciously consumed as much information as I could about sensory issues. In 2010, most of what I could find online and in books was geared towards parents of young children with SPD or was written specifically for the children themselves. I grimaced as I followed the dotted lines of a sensory activity book meant for someone 20 years my junior. It was frustrating to be so close to the material, to have it be so relatable in general, and yet to still feel like a misfit. I had to dismiss the silly thought I kept having that I was the one and only adult with sensory issues, the one outlier, like Bigfoot.

During this time, I was in a master's program for mental health counseling, an interest that had developed after so much exposure to psychotherapy during my adolescence and early adulthood. I found that the more I learned about what mental health issues looked like, the more I understood the similarities to my sensory issues as well as the crucial differences. I also found another adult with SPD, my friend Dan Travis, and with his welcoming support and willingness to compare notes, I felt way less alone. I started chronicling my experiences though evaluation and treatment as well as during my daily life—not unlike how an old-timey sailing ship's captain kept an ongoing log for later reflection once he'd reached shore. I fondly call this part of my life *coming to my senses*, which is also the name of my blog about my journey. It was as if in one moment I was wading through the dark muck, and in the next, I had burst forth into this clarity about who I was and what I was undergoing.

I thought that maybe my blog could also serve as a guidepost for other weary sensory travelers, if there were any, to remind them that, although the journey of an undiagnosed sensory life feels long and painful, they weren't alone. To be honest, I never expected anyone else to traverse the same sands. At the time, there weren't any other strict SPD-only blogs written by fellow adults. I never would have guessed that a mere few years later, people would find their way to me and come to their own senses because of my blog. I always loved setting an example and being a mentor and teacher. Every single time someone thanks me for writing about sensory issues, I am reminded that, although I have struggled for years to understand myself and to be understood by others, it has been worth every single second of my life's challenges to help bring someone else clarity—much like Dan did for me when I was lost and scared.

People always ask me why I'm so open and willing to share intimate details about my life and experiences, especially when it leaves me open and exposed to barbs and criticisms. I keep few things about myself private. While it's true that I have a background in both writing and mental health and I also happen to have sensory issues, I believe that the role of sensory adults is to be the mouthpiece for the sensory community and to bring attention to our cause. Back when I was younger, I could've used someone on the inside who understood my particular struggles. Someone who knew what it felt like to startle at even the tiniest change in lighting or cry in the presence of dozens of undulating bodies walking through the human circus that is Times Square to corroborate my unusual stories and help me persuade others that I had something going on inside of me that was worth their consideration. As children, we don't have the words that we need to express how we're feeling. My childhood "I don't feel good" (never "well," mind you—desperate times called for garbled English) became the only phrase I had to highlight that I was feeling overstimulated and detached. Adults with sensory issues finally have adequate words to describe these crucial and otherwise hidden experiences—words that have taken years to form. We can use our experiences as a critical teaching tool to educate all facets of our community, as well as the global community, about the major issues that impact and sometimes necessarily dictate our lives.

There's so much to say about sensory issues, and what I've laid out in this book only scratches the surface. In the chapters that follow, I share with you what I believe to be the most important points in this field in order to have a working knowledge of what it means to be a person living in a sensory world with sensory issues. I'm not an occupational therapist. I'm not a researcher. I'm a mental health counselor, advocate, writer, and your newest compassionate sensory friend. I'm a woman who somehow found herself turning over all available rocks looking for uncomplicated answers to explain a lifetime of bumps and bruises. I want to simplify the sensory world for you so that even the least sensory sensitive reader can understand the most complex sensory battle. We no longer have to fear the things we have yet to understand.

So let me be your ultimate example—as you already know, I surely don't mind sharing! I turn myself over to you fully, atypical neurology and all. Dissect the sinew on your mark. Let me help you make sense of sensory issues.

How Not to Read This Book:

I have little patience for intolerance—you can say I'm intolerant of intolerance (how hipster of me). People with sensory issues, be they Sensory Processing Disorder or Autism Spectrum Disorder in nature, deal with enough misunderstanding, teasing, self-deprecation, and physical symptoms for ten lifetimes. As humans, we often ridicule what we don't understand or what we fear. Guess what, you can't catch sensory issues, and I'm about to help you understand the things you don't yet know, so put away those derogatory terms and thoughts. No excuses here, sayeth this sensory gatekeeper. Also, the information I've included is not only super-important for your understanding, it's also correct to the best of my knowledge and from my personal experiences as a sensory person and an advocate in touch with many sensory people. I say this because sometimes there are still some discrepancies in this field, especially between what research has found and what is done in practice as well as from one person's understanding of an idea to the next. The brain is the next frontier of science, and we have to have patience not only with missing proof but also with slight variations on what we see and know to reach similar results. As more and more people talk about sensory issues, these disparities will become smaller and smaller until we're all finally in alignment. All opinions are important, including my own.

Chapter 2 ❧

Living in a Sensory World

Let's try something here. Take a second to shut your eyes tightly, hold your hands firmly against your ears, and step away from anything your body might be inadvertently touching. If you're feeling adventurous, only breathe through your mouth. It's too bad you can't be easily suspended above the ground, because really—that would help me make this point. Obviously make sure you're not standing on the platform waiting for a train or about to bungee jump off a cliff before doing all of this. Let's not play in traffic, children! Spend a good minute looking like a Hear No Evil, See No Evil, Speak No Evil monkey before dropping your hands to your side and opening up those peepers. I'll wait for you to finish ...

Author's Note #1: If this book were a song, now would be its musical interlude.
Author's Note #2: I'll give a prize to the first person who turns this book into a song.

Welcome back. Now take a minute and really look around you. See how the gently dipping sunlight paints dappled shadows on your kitchen walls. See how the communal office printer subtly shakes your padded, beige cubicle walls when there's a job in its queue. Listen, like a human satellite dish, to the waves of sound in your immediate sphere. Hear the faint hum of a bumblebee as it passes by a crisp green stalk of blue hydrangea, and the din of people mid-stride and mid-conversation as they cross the next big avenue. Feel your body leaning against that concrete pillar, your feet planted firmly on the muddy ground, your cold and ungloved hands as they graze each blade of grass in the early hours of spring.

Like it or not, we are all firmly fixed in a sensory world. Your local baker, the elderly woman next door, the president, even you and me—we're all sensory beings. In order to be a person living in your body, you are required to engage with the world outside. Imagine a life in which you are unable to externalize beyond your thoughts—a strange town where the population is always just you. You swirl around this plane of musings and theories without

ever feeling linked to anyone or anything in particular. You can't turn inward to meet your basic needs, like shelter, safety, or food (last I checked, Youville has no 24-hour diner, sorry for the inconvenience). Without the external world, the physical human body would cease to exist, and the mind would have no inner life. We need the sensory world because we're intimately intertwined with the sensory world.

Always desperate to exist in this sphere, the main areas that constitute our basic needs are rich with sensory information. We smear colorful paints on the walls of our home and strategically place lighting, objects, and photographs to catch the attention of our guests and evoke pleasant feelings. Parties in these spaces are choreographed dances of sounds, sights, and tastes. We eat food that appeals to us not only in flavor but also in texture and in smell. We swirl glasses of red wine and dip our noses deeply into the glass, breathing in the woody aromas; we sip and taste. We burn our hands on the stovetop and yank the tender flesh quickly away from the fiery range.

Even our common greeting customs are like leaps outward. Although these habits vary slightly, there is a global trend of pressing our hands, bodies, or lips together in some combination. Saying hello and goodbye—bringing ourselves into a common space with someone else for a period of time and then parting ways—is interestingly enough a very sensory experience. Have you ever noticed your client's rough hand in yours? The sweaty-palmed shake of your last date? Even the least intimate of gestures, the handshake, is a plunge into sensory waters, and this makes sense. You can't shake hands with someone's brain. As we don't share space in our minds, we share space in the world outside of our bodies.

People with impairments to one or more of the sensory organs find doorways to the outside as well. In 1887, Helen Keller, famed blind and deaf author, speaker, suffragette, and humanitarian, was finally reached by her teacher, Anne Sullivan, through touch. She experienced the feeling of water flowing through her hands and connected the physical object to the word signed into her palm—something she called a "living word." The word was brought to life by the sensory experience it represented. Helen Keller is one of my favorite examples of a successful life in a sensory world in spite of sensory challenges. In her autobiography, she describes the word water as having woken up her soul, but in reality, it gave her a way to connect to the world outside of her being.

Recent studies have shown that, when one sense is lost or missing, the brain re-purposes the areas typically used for one sense to boost another. It's not that being deaf means we have naturally heightened other senses; our brain just learns how to support the other senses differently. Our body and our brain clearly want us to participate in the sensory world. Although the portals change based on the person and their physical makeup, the urge to reach outward and connect is innate.

In case you're still not convinced, blink. We carry convenient little portals to the outside right on our faces and bodies. Our eyes, ears, mouth, nose, and skin act like doorways to connect us to our planet and to one another. Some say that the eyes are the windows to the soul, but I'd say that the eyes and the other sense organs are the windows to our life. Pull the toggle of the shades and let them slip upwards, and you can see, hear, touch, smell, taste, and feel your body at rest and in motion.

Whether you're a homebody or a social butterfly, gazing across the living room or surveying the crowd at a concert, walking down a hallway or striding through the busy streets of New York City, your sensory experiences create the ambiance of the life you lead. They shape us at our very core and determine the path our life will take. We are who we are because of the things we've experienced. Lived through a train wreck? Listened to your favorite poet read his favorite poem live? Heard your firstborn cry for the first time? Watched your beloved grandparent die? Met your hero? Everything that we do in the sensory world has the power to influence our internal state of being and the direction in which we move as we grow. We wake up, humming some unnamed tune, reviewing the details of a dream like a newsreel, scratching errant patches of sunburn from a day at the beach. Perhaps we feel calm and soothed from the hours spent by the ocean, or transformed by someone we met while sprawled out on the sand. It may be less significant than, say, the rush you experienced when you first plummeted downward on a rollercoaster, or the intense reverberation in every cell when you fell in love for the first time—less memorable, but it invokes feelings and memories nonetheless, connections to the present and the past. It leaves a mark of some kind. Like Pink Floyd sang, "All you touch and all you see/is all your life will ever be."

Chapter 3
The Senses, Demystified

M. Night Shyamalan was wrong—in sensory circles, at least. I'm no Ebert. When he named his dramatic 1999 mystery-thriller film, *The Sixth Sense*, he clearly hadn't spoken to anyone remotely knowledgeable about neurology.

Actually, most of what we learned in grade school about the senses is incomplete. Sure, we have five senses, but that's like saying we have nine months in a year. It's not technically wrong. I mean, we do in fact have nine months in a year—but they are part of a larger set of twelve. Skip a few months and you're not looking at a full year.

Just like we actually have twelve months, according to many professionals in the sensory field, we actually have—are you ready for this? EIGHT senses. Not five. Eight. Yes, I know, I just blew your mind. Is everything you've ever known about your senses now in question? Probably. To be clear, that eight is not counting M. Night Shyamalan's "sixth" sense, the one that may or may not allow us to perceive the unseen world. We're talking about eight, very real, very legitimate ways to engage with the sensory world and our internal self. (And note, some researchers call out more than twenty senses—but to be honest, I believe in the eight I'm about to list because I know from experience how complex life can be when each one isn't processed right. Experiencing is everything, sometimes.)

Sensation and Perception:

When we think about the senses, we're talking about both "sensation" and "perception." "Sensation" is the physical act of the sensory organs being stimulated by the environment, while "perception" is the mental process of interpreting and processing the information taken in by the sense organs. The eyes see (that's sensation), but then the brain processes what the eyes have seen and assigns meaning to the information and helps us determine our response (that's perception). People with sensory issues usually don't have issues with sensation, but they struggle with perception and responding appropriately to what the brain perceives.

Let's start with the ones you probably already know.

Sight

Whether or not you can see, you're undoubtedly familiar with this sense. With our sight, we can distinguish light and darkness, colors and shadows, textures and distance. We can gauge the emotional reactions of others by watching their body language. I am looking at my computer screen as I type these exact words, and there's a good chance that you're using your eyes to read them.

What most people consider "vision" is actually visual perception, or the interpretation of our environment though the processing of the information that we take in through our eyes to the brain. It's not just eyesight. A person with sensory issues can have normal visual acuity (or what we call 20-20 vision) and can be unable to process visual information accurately due to how his brain is wired. Within the whole wide light spectrum, humans are able to take in only visible light, which is a very small segment of the spectrum. Light comes into the eye as visual information and is turned into neural impulses, which are electrical signals that are sent to the brain for processing and translation. It's the brain's job to take the signals and make sense of them, much like a computer transforms haphazard code into meaningful, usable programs.

Seeing allows us to make sense of the things we're witnessing and determine the next action we need to take—whether physical or mental. If you see your mother emerging from customs after a long flight dragging her suitcase behind her, and she catches your eye and excitedly waves, unless you have some longstanding emotional issues or have recently broken your arm, you will probably excitedly wave back at her. She hasn't said a word to you just yet, and you haven't come into physical contact with her, but thanks to your visual perception, you know she is in the same space, you can gauge how she is feeling about being in your presence by interpreting the expression on her face, and you can meet her gesture with an appropriate response.

Research shows that 80-85% of our learning, perception, and cognition activities come to us through our vision. As with each sense, its ultimate purpose is to help us survive. Visual perception helps us to find food and shelter as well as avoid predators, but vision's basic, specific biological purpose is to help us navigate through space. Many babies who are visually impaired do not crawl or explore their surroundings in the same way as sighted babies and often omit crawling entirely and head directly into walking. As we develop from birth to about age 8 or 9, we move from interpreting our world through motor and tactile cues (what a baby's doing when she pops a LEGO Duplo block into her mouth—it's not because the red squares tastes like cherry ices, trust me) and become more directed by vision. After that age, because we've experienced more of our surroundings, we're better able to rely on visual cues to understand our world, and we don't need to chew on, say, a doctor's stethoscope to know what the tool is and how it'll be used. (If you want to nibble on a hard copy of this book or are actively trying to gnaw on your e-Reader as we speak, there's no shame, really. I'll look the other way.)

Hearing

Another pivotal sense, hearing, is both obviously and subtly powerful. Like seeing, hearing is more than just the act of listening. Auditory processing is how the brain interprets the meaning behind sound. Ears detect the vibration of noises and voices in the air and turn them into electrical impulses for processing by the brain. We glean important clues about our sensory world through our ears, especially when they relate to staying safe and meeting our basic needs. Hearing is the only sensory system that connects us to our entire immediate environment at once. We have to look at an object or person to see them, but we can hear the noises that they make regardless of where they are in relation to our bodies. This is especially useful when it comes to unseen threats to our survival, like a wild animal lurking in the woods. We may not have eyes in the back of our head, but thankfully we have ears to fill us in about what we can't see.

Auditory processing also allows us to engage fully in speech, enabling us to easily communicate with one another for social and educational purposes. Speech and music are emotional and very personal components of the human experience. Studies have shown that, around the seventh and eighth months of life, the heartbeat of babies in utero slows down in response to their mother's voice, and once born, babies will continue to recognize this voice. Scour the Internet, and you can watch dozens of (supremely touching) videos showing deaf adults, children, and infants hearing voices for the first time, thanks to the support of implants and aids. One 9-week-old deaf boy looks genuinely surprised at the sound emanating from his mother's mouth and smiles and coos in response to her murmurs, and a young deaf woman hears her own voice for the first time and cries. Feel the warmth spreading throughout your body when you hear the familiar voice of a loved one, and you know that speech is a powerful, meaningful force.

As for music, a fantastic *Scientific American* article from 2009, "Why Does Music Make Us Feel?" by Mark Changizi, explores the possibility that music is an abstract form of language—although, the author points out, most of the emotion of abstract language is in the meaning of the words chosen. Someone singing in a language that we don't understand won't evoke as much emotion within us as someone singing in our own language. He also suggests that music is like a summary of our expressive movements. Our auditory system helps us to make sense of the movements of those in our environment, and some of these movements are interpreted as positive, while others act as warning signals about our immediate safety. The sound of soft, paced padding across the floor might mean that your partner is coming to bed, while the sound of a tense, barking dog might mean that you could get bitten. We naturally gravitate towards the more joyful sounds, as they trigger positive emotions.

Touch

Touch is part of a complex system involving receptors in the skin that detect everything from temperature to pressure. After a touch, these receptors send information in the form of electrical signals to the spinal cord and the brain, where the meaning behind the signal is processed and interpreted.

Touch is one of the first sensory systems to develop. While it isn't considered as crucial as sight and sound for active survival purposes, this primitive sense is a necessary part of the human experience. Touch enables us to connect to one another and establish physical and emotional bonds. The temperature of a mother's chest is a few degrees warmer than the rest of her body after she has given birth, encouraging touch between the mom and her newborn. The temperature of a mother's body has also been found to fluctuate based on her baby's temperature needs, making touch a more subtle survival tool. Touch also plays an important role in development. Newborns need the stimulation of touch to engage some of their basic reflexes, like the rooting reflex, which assists with feeding. Touch—especially with the mouth—allows infants to learn about their world.

Children born into deprived settings sometimes must learn to thrive without adequate touch and emotional connection. Observing these children, we can see just how important it is to touch and be touched during early childhood. Studies conducted by Nathan Fox and his colleagues at the University of Maryland about Romanian orphanages in the 1980s found that many children had increased levels of stress hormones as well as decreased hormones linked to emotional and social bonding. Although these levels were shown to fluctuate somewhat when kids were moved from orphanages into family homes, the switch couldn't fully undo the early damage done from inconsistent touch.

At the other end of life's spectrum, touch reduces the levels of stress hormones in Alzheimer's patients. However, the sense of touch also deteriorates with age. Studies show that we lose one percent of our tactile sense every year after age 18 thanks to the decrease of the density of nerve endings in our hands as well as the slowed pace of tactile information reaching the brain. Some people attribute the frequent falls of the elderly to the decreased sense of touch on the soles of their feet.

Touch is also a powerful form of non-verbal communication. It allows us to express different emotions through a simple act. A touch on the arm can be romantic or consoling, based on the context of the conversation. Punch someone in the face, and it's clear that you're probably not congratulating him on the latest addition to his family. Shove him, and you're clearly not apologizing for clocking him on the nose.

Taste

Taste is yet another example of sensation vs. perception (if you missed the definition of these two terms, flip back to page 20. While receptor cells in our taste buds perform the physical act of sensing taste, it is once again the brain that assigns meaning to taste, thanks to three specialized taste nerves that send messages to the brain for translation. Is the chard too salty? Too bitter? Don't ask your tongue.

Taste, like the other senses, has a primal purpose—it's like a guide, an important tool for staying well. What we eat literally defines whether or not we survive. If we make a mistake and accidentally eat something poisonous, we're as good as gone. Along with smell, what we taste acts as a clue to how we might handle the nutrients or chemicals we're about to digest. Typically, foods that both taste and smell bad are spoiled and not for consumption (woe to the lonely Durian fruit, a Southeast Asia native that tastes nutty and custardy—that is if you can get past its smell of rotting flesh). We're typically attracted to sweet and salty foods—sweet for its carbohydrates, which we use for energy, and salty because sodium is crucial for cellular function and neural communication. (Side-note: salt is so important to our wellbeing that the word "salary," which is the money that sustains our lifestyle, comes from the Latin *salarium*, or "payment in salt.")

Newborns already have a fully developed sense of taste—aside from salt, which isn't perceived until a baby is four months old. In utero, fetuses taste the amniotic fluid surrounding them, and when they're born, newborns are immediately more attracted to sweet flavors. Like the other senses, taste declines to some degree as we get older—specifically after age 50. Scientists are not entirely sure why, but it may have something to do with the decrease in the sense of smell. (More on smell shortly.) People who lose their sense of taste due to old age, injury, medication, or a medical condition also often lose their appetite, which affects the amount of vitamins and minerals they consume. Food without taste really is a meaningless mouthful of random textures.

Smell

The sensation of smell takes place in our nose, where odor molecules drift into the nasal cavity, and receptor cells send signals to the brain for identification. Smell is the first sense we use when we're born. Newborns not only can recognize the smell of amniotic fluid, they are also soothed by the scents they experience immediately after birth. Studies show that newborns within a week of birth can also identify the smell of their mothers, and their sense of smell helps them as they learn to feed.

Smell also plays a key role in ensuring our survival. Like the sense of taste, smell alerts us to spoiled or poisonous food as well as to hazards that we can't detect with any other sense. Anyone who's ever smelled gas in the house knows how truly important this sense is when it comes to hidden, invisible dangers. Foul smells are even sent as pain signals to the brain to stress the importance of correcting the potentially problematic situation.

The sense of smell acts like a portal to our memories. Catch a faint whiff of lemon or spice, and you're suddenly seventeen again, nose-deep in your high school boyfriend's sweatshirt. This is probably because the area of the brain that processes smell is part of a larger area that also processes emotion and is responsible for associative learning. We link smells to events, places, people, or things—what is called a "conditioned response"—especially when we're young, as we're exposed to many smells for the first time in childhood. Let's say that, when you were a kid, your sweet, white-haired great-grandma always baked cookies when you visited. There she stood alongside the oven, red pot-holder in hand, ready to retrieve the buttery, sugary morsels. You'd burn your mouth on the mounds of dough, you were just that excited to bite into the rounds. You'd laugh, she'd laugh, and you'd get a kiss on your forehead when you were through. As an adult, you'd probably think of your great-grandma each time you smelled baking cookies—or even if she didn't spring to mind, you might feel calm and safe, much like you did when you were little and in her care. The smell of cookies would always evoke memories of that happy, innocent time.

Smell also plays a role in our attraction to one another. Odorless and in-visible chemicals called pheromones are produced by the body and released through sweat and other bodily fluids. Pheromones are sensed by the nose much like other smells, yet the information is processed in the areas of the brain that deal with emotion and desire. Pheromones act as a means of com-munication. Female pheromones raise male testosterone, and male phero-mones gently stimulate the production of hormones in women with the ulti-mate purpose of ... um ... well, you know.

I'm sure that most of that information was at least somewhat familiar to you. We're very quick to talk about the first five senses, and less quick to understand the remaining three. Although they're less obvious (or, rather, not as plain as the nose on your face—*snicker*), they also ultimately have a significant impact on people with sensory issues.

Proprioception—Our Bodies in Space

Pronounced PRO-pree-oh-SEP-shun (I've even heard PRO-PRYO-SEP-shun—but really, *tomayto, tomahto*), this is the sense of our body's position, location, and orientation in physical space. *Proprioceptors*, or the cells that sense proprioception, are located in our muscles and joints, and when we move, they send information to the brain for processing about the position of our body and each related limb. Because of this sense, we can control our limbs without looking down at them with every complex series of motions. If you can cook, drive, play sports, walk the dog down the street, change the channel on the TV, give a high-five, or do anything involving the motion of your body, you intimately know proprioception.

Proprioception can be called the "grand modulator of the nervous system." It tells us where we end—the edge of our physical being—and where the world begins. It calms us down when we are all energized, because it's calming to know where our body is in space. It gives our physical being meaning and connects us to the planet that we inhabit. Proprioception also hypes us up when we're feeling lethargic. Know that feeling when you finally scrape your corporal being off of the couch and take a walk? Sure, it feels great because the wind is in your hair, nature is at play, society is unfolding before you (if you like these sorts of things, that is—I just described a probable sensory nightmare!), but it also feels great because you're connected physically to your body and your environment.

It's not just the physical connection, though. Input to our joints and muscles via movement increases levels of serotonin within our bodies, a chemical made by the body to help regulate our mood. It also regulates other similar

chemicals, like dopamine, the famous "reward" chemical—which is more related to unexpected rewards—so we're not driven to seek non-stop pleasure.
Ever noticed that you're less likely to inhale a whole bag of chips after going
to the gym? You can thank that good proprioceptive input you got while
running on the treadmill.

We take this sense for granted, but most people are unfamiliar with the
term. (Even the software I'm using to write this book doesn't recognize the
word; for shame!) It allows us to perform the seemingly most simple of actions
without noticing our body or where our body is located in space. Near a wall?
A person? Outdoors? I'd bet you rarely detect these minute details before starting an action. You probably can complete an entire physical movement without
smashing into something in your space. It truly is such a pivotal, subtle sense—
one that you surely only notice when it's missing or not functioning.

Vestibular—Balance

The vestibular system is located in the inner ear and deals with balance,
orientation, and our position relative to gravity. In sensory circles, we think
of this as the most important sense because we can't make any physical movements on this planet that aren't governed by gravity. The vestibular sense
affects muscle tone (so we stay upright), visual-motor control (so we don't fall
down stairs), visual-spatial perception (so we can navigate through the dark),
and the ability to keep us alert and attentive.

Aside from the sense of smell, our vestibular system works hand in hand with
many of our other senses. Walking down stairs, for example, is a multi-sensory
effort between our balance, proprioception, and sight. Having trouble with one
of these three senses doesn't rule out our ability to head down the stairs, but it
makes the act more complicated. Sight, for example, can guide us if our vestibular sense is struggling, but sight can't tell us some crucial information about

our environment, like whether or not we're actually on flat ground. This makes the vestibular sense especially important—none of the other senses can work enough in tandem to make up for what's missing if it's not functioning properly. If we're without vision, we can listen to the sounds within the environment, feel balanced and discern where we are in space, use our sense of touch to define the outlines of objects, and bring in smell and taste as needed to further refine what we think we're experiencing. But if our vestibular sense goes, we're without data on how to move safely through our space. (The same can also be said of proprioception, which, when gone, leaves a person feeling disconnected from the ground and environment.)

Interoception—Our Internal Sense

It's noon in Theoretical Town, and you finally look up from your work laptop long enough to realize that it's time for a break. You stand, stretch, and head to the restroom before grabbing some lunch. Once outside, it's so windy that you wish you'd taken your sweater. Shivering, you pick up a sandwich at the deli, look down at your watch, and realize that you're late for a conference call. You dart back to the office, food in hand, and reach your desk just in time. As you dial in, you unwrap your sandwich and catch your breath.

Hungry? Cold? Sleepy? Have a racing heart? Need to use the bathroom? You know how your body is feeling thanks to our eighth sense, interoception. This sense is key to our day-to-day functioning as a person living within a body. It helps us identify the state of our organs and what needs to be done to maintain homeostasis, or a balanced state. Internal sensors, like nerve endings that line the respiratory and digestive systems, send signals to the brain for interpretation about our inner, physical function needs.

Most of us barely ever think about this sense or would have even considered this to be a sense without my pointing it out. Sure, we sense that we're hungry, so we go eat. We feel the need to go to the bathroom, and, well, we go. If our heart is racing, we slow down and take a pause. We're typically able to accommodate interoception without having a full, meaningful conversation with the sense. When we smell something delicious, we might stop in our tracks to figure out what we're detecting, where it's coming from, and how we can finagle a bite for ourselves. With interoception, it's more automatic or reactive. Our body tells us what it needs, and we seek to meet those needs without question or discussion.

Like proprioception and the vestibular sense, interoception becomes more obvious when its functioning is impaired—probably because the sense organs in question are less prominent or never seen, even by us. It's clear when our hearing or sight is impacted, but less obvious to onlookers when it's something we're sensing inside only. It's also harder for a person to recognize that what he has felt internally for his entire life is not what most people feel inside. Doctors check vision and hearing, but they can't check these three final senses, whose impacts can only really be identified internally by the individual.

Chapter 4 ᵔᵔᵔ

Sensory Issues, Clarified

If life were simple, you'd now know everything about the senses, and this guidebook would be super short (or not needed at all, but don't tell my publisher!).

You know that:

1. We are beings living in a sensory world.
2. We have sensory organs.
3. We have eight senses.
4. We sense and process sensory information from said world with said organs.

For many people, this four-part list is their entire sensory experience. It's all the information they need to understand their sensory lives. If this is you and this is your ultimate goal, that's totally fine. Judgment-free author is judgment free! Shut the book and keep walking into the distance, I'll stand here waving until you're just a small blip on the horizon.

For some of us, however, this four-part list is just the very beginning. It's the once upon a time of our life story, the foundation upon which our true complexities unfold. Sure, we are beings living in a sensory world. Sure, we have sensory organs and eight senses. However, some of us also have sensory issues.

So what do I mean when I say "sensory issues"? I mean that sometimes, although someone is sensing typically (like hearing, for example), he or she does not perceive or interpret the information in a typical way. The perception is completely unrelated to the sense organs, like the nose or the eyes, and related instead to the brain itself and how it interprets the sensory input it receives. I may hear a sound completely fine within the structure of my ear, but once the sound turns into an electrical impulse and hits my brain, I'm not translating the sound properly into a meaningful identification and reaction. An ice cream truck's cheery ring—again, heard typically by my ears—might be processed by my brain as a loud, shrill, and almost threatening siren.

As sensing humans, we're like audio technicians with a soundboard. Many people without sensory issues have brains that can keep the knobs at a tolerable middle level, which is typical for most people. Those of us with sensory issues, either just SPD or a diagnosis on *the spectrum* (i.e. an Autism Spectrum Disorder [ASD], which in recent medical and diagnostic manuals also includes *Asperger's syndrome*, a condition that many still believe should be its own unique diagnosis), have a different kind of soundboard, maybe even another brand. Our dials are always turned way up or way down, and it's difficult and often impossible to regulate these switches.

A Word about My Aspie Friends:

I like to think that the greater sensory community is composed of three general subgroups: people with SPD, people with an ASD, and people with Asperger's syndrome. Asperger's syndrome is technically a subset of autism. Although the condition includes many of the social and emotional challenges that are often seen in autism (as well as the sensory sensitivities seen in SPD), Aspies rarely experience any of the language delays prevalent in autism. Many Aspies are even considered verbally preco-cious, using grown-up speech years before their peers.

In asking a well-respected Aspie advocate and friend of mine about the condi-tion, she said, "of course, SPD comes as a free, bonus extension pack when you have Asperger's," sending me into a giggle-fit. That says it all ... and so cleverly, too.

Asperger's first appeared in the American Psychiatric Association's Diagnostic and Statistical Manual of Mental Disorders (DSM) in the book's fourth iteration in 1994 as its own discrete disorder. In the latest version of the DSM, Asperger's syn-drome was folded into the general diagnosis of an ASD. I've heard from some Aspies who are disillusioned to see their diagnosis, and therefore a tangible piece of their identity, blended into something else and given a different clinical name. My Aspie advocate friend told me that she and many others are comfortable with this shift and consider themselves to be on the autism spectrum anyhow.

Regardless of the DSM's classification of Asperger's syndrome, it clearly still exists. We must continue to honor the Aspies in our lives by using whatever term they feel most comfortable with to describe their experience of the world.

There are three major categories of SPD called *subtypes*, and these cate-gories have several subtypes. They're very complicated but all meaningful to understand. Someone with sensory issues may experience some degree of each of them, or just one or two.

People with SPD may have ...

1. Sensory Modulation Disorder
2. Sensory Discrimination Disorder
3. Sensory-Based Motor Disorder

Sensory Modulation Disorder

People with *Sensory Modulation Disorder* have trouble *modulating* or *regulating* sensory information. They (although this is what I primarily have, so I should say we) tend to respond to sensory input in three ways:

1. They CRAVE input from one or more of the senses (also called "craving")

2. They AVOID input from one or more of the senses (also called "over-responsivity")

3. They IGNORE input from one or more of the senses (also called "under-responsivity")

CRAVE

Imagine perpetually needing bright lights or strong smells to feel your best. Picture the desire to be jostled and tossed around, to touch and be touched by loved ones and strangers, to have all dials turned up to be the loudest, brightest, boldest, and most vivid in order for you to feel calm and poised. This is what it's like to be a craver of a particular kind of sensory input.

Although I mostly fall under the AVOID category and am classified as "over-responsive" to most sensations, I am someone who perpetually seeks touch. If I'm not running my fingers along the wall as I walk down a corridor, I'm tracing circles on our microsuede couch or playing with people's hair. I've described my fingertips as hungry. There are seemingly not enough soft, cold things in the world for me to touch—I'm rarely (never?) satisfied, and so I am constantly and ravenously searching for velveteen and fur.

A person who CRAVES input from a sense (or multiple senses) may prefer his or her world to have an abundance of these sensations to feel calm and centered:

Sight — bright, undulating, colorful, novel

Hearing — loud, layering, from a broad range, musical

Touch — soft, textured

Taste — strong, bold

Smell — strong, sharp, or unfamiliar

Vestibular — moving, energetic, thrilling

Proprioception — tight, deep input (like hugs)

Interoception — heart pounding, intensely hungry, deep breaths

AVOID

Imagine the loudest, brightest, busiest, most in-motion scenario of your life (the type of place that our sensory craving friend above might enjoy). Maybe you're a New Yorker like me and have been to Times Square at night. Maybe you've been to a packed music festival like Coachella. Try to envision a place of ceaseless, bullying information—so complex and intertwined that you can't parse a shriek from a flash of light. It's incoherent and confusing—and take it from me, it actually hurts. This is life with sensory modulation problems when you're over-responsive.

A person who AVOIDS input from a sense (or multiple senses) may prefer his or her world to have one (or a handful) of these aspects to feel calm and centered:

Sight — dim or dark lighting, everyone and everything in slow motion, plain and simple, familiar

Hearing — quiet, no variation in sound

Touch — no touching or less touching by loved ones and especially strangers, predictable touch

Taste — plain and familiar flavors

Smell — no obvious smells or only familiar smells

Vestibular — no motion, low energy, mellow

Proprioception — loose clothing, no heavy lifting

Interoception — no excitement, frequent meals and bathroom breaks

Being bombarded by the senses when you're over-responsive can be a terrifying experience. When we're overtaken with an influx of sensory information, we sensitive folk are not unlike a drowning man out at sea while caught in an engulfing rainstorm. Each piece of sensory input—from the feel of our feet on the floor to the laugh of a stranger—cascades upon us without our consent, and we must constantly fight to keep our heads above water. Many typically wired people have a mutual relationship with their senses at all times—they let information in and keep information out—yet those like me are doormats, especially without treatment, tools, exercises, or the basic understanding of ourselves and our situation; the sensory world is always standing on us and aggressively pounding down our doors. I personally believe that life can be frustrating and challenging for people with all types of SPD, and I also believe that the most sensory-sensitive of us, stuck between unyielding input and a brain that won't process properly, have extra special challenges.

I speak from experience here. Although I do seek and ignore some input, I am an avid avoider of all things loud, bright, tight, and fast. (See that balled up lump of flesh in the corner? It's me with my eyes closed and my hands clamped over my ears, chanting, "no no no no no no.")

In my life as an SPD advocate, most of the people that I meet have over-responsive sensory modulation issues—way more than any other sub-type. The sensitivity associated with those who are over-responsive is usually pretty intense. We "sensory sensitives" are challenged to function well in an environment that feels particularly overwhelming much of the time and operates on a much more concentrated level than we're able to tolerate effectively without intervention.

While someone who seeks input may feel at home in this electronic age of social media, constant engagement may prove especially difficult for us avoiders who feel our best in a quieter, dimmer, slower-paced environment. It's more obvious to people with this particular subtype of SPD that something's going on within them, and so they're quicker to realize that they need help.

It's also important for you to know that people with modulation issues may not perceive some of the senses as problematic at all while also perceiving others as incredibly debilitating. Personally, I rarely have an issue with smell, yet without fail, I always have sensitivities related to sight and sound. There's also no telling what combination of senses will be impacted or which one of the three variations listed in the modulation category (crave, avoid, ignore) will pair with which sense. Will the person crave smell? Avoid proprioception? Ignore sound? Have no issue with balance? This varies from person to person. Very few people have the same exact sensory issues, making this condition especially unique.

IGNORE

People who are under-responsive to sensory input may not notice happenings in the sensory world, or they might react to them super-slowly. The traditional world of someone with mostly under-responsivity isn't pressured with the almost blinding, driving need to engage or disengage. For under-responders, it takes extra engagement from the senses to get their attention. Unlike cravers, whose war cry is *All the input will be mine!*, they don't have a gnawing drive to be showered with sensory information. Unlike avoiders, whose war cry is *Flee the input!*, they aren't trying to tuck their heads into the proverbial sands of solitude. This under-responsivity is more of a neutral, passive environment in which many things just don't register as quickly. Clothing may be twisted on the body and look a little sloppy, and the person may not jump when they hear someone shout their name. Their war cry is simply, *Huh?*

It can be scary when you're aware that you're so unaware. Take me, for example. I am under-responsive to proprioception. My body and brain are clueless when it comes to this sense (I am rarely, if ever, tethered to the space around me), and I can't discern where my physical being ends and where the world begins. This is why I also crave touch. I am actively looking to find my edges.

Poor proprioception means that I am supremely accident-prone and always covered in mysterious bruises, and I am well aware that my brain doesn't recognize proprioceptive input. I almost watch my brain failing to connect my body to the ground and to the environment, and I hold my breath. I know that I am likely to completely misgauge the distance between my body and the curb and stumble into the street. If there's a knife in the vicinity, you can bet that I will somehow end up cut and bleeding. (I once somehow dropped a knife as I attempted to cut a lemon, managing to plunge the sharp tip right into the top of my bare foot. Just one story of hundreds in the personal annals of *Where Am I, Dammit: The Rachel S. Schneider Story.*) While I spend a great deal of time running away from some input and running toward other input, I wish upon all the stars in our galaxy that I could feel secure in my body moving through space. It's something people without sensory issues must take for granted—the simple pleasure of really being somewhere, not just in mind and soul but also in a well-informed, well-wired brain and body.

People with under-responsivity issues may also have a complex relationship with pain. Unable to feel the full extent of pain, it could take more force—more burning, more sharpness, more ache—for them to register that they have a problem. This high threshold of pain tolerance can be dangerous and cause extensive injury if the under-responsive person doesn't take extra precautions. I can relate to this, too. Let me just say that my tenure doing yoga (which I loved) was sadly cut short by a crazy, major back injury. In a body so removed from the proprioceptive present, it's no wonder that I ended up arched backward in screaming pain. Being oblivious is not always such a blessing.

Sensory Discrimination Disorder

Others deal with issues in the second category, *Sensory Discrimination Disorder*, which includes the difficulty of understanding the basic sensory qualities of people, places, objects, or the environment. In this category, a person may have trouble figuring out the source of a sound; the feel of an object without looking at it directly; and how much pressure to apply when holding, lifting, or using an object without breaking it. In a bustling world filled with sensory information, discrimination allows us to sort through it all quickly and respond to it properly. When all is well, it helps us clue in to the people, objects, and places with which we interact.

People with both discrimination issues and modulation issues may be less aware of the discrimination problems, and instead only focus on correcting their issues with modulation. For example, if someone has trouble figuring out where a sound is coming from and also has difficulty processing and reacting to the auditory input because she is so very over-responsive, there's a chance that she'll notice her discrimination issue less because it's not so painful and focus more on the modulation sensitivity. While I usually can't tell where a sound is coming from (I'm that person who pivots the complete opposite way from a sound, desperately seeking a source), it has very little bearing on my life. I can laugh off my inability to find the source of a sound or shrug when I need both my hands and my eyes to find something in my purse, but I absolutely cannot dismiss my sensory modulation issues.

Sensory-Based Motor Disorder

Some people with sensory issues struggle with either maintaining posture (a difficulty called "postural disorder") or the planning and executing of movements to complete a task (called "dyspraxia"). These two subtypes comprise the third category, *Sensory-Based Motor Disorder*, and are more focused on *motor coordination* (or the coordination of body movement) and balance, which involves proprioception, vestibular processing, and touch.

People with motor issues are stuck in a body that doesn't always do what their brains ask. Things like hand-eye coordination, handwriting, balance while standing, and sitting upright in a chair can be nightmarish hellscapes. Feeling clumsy and uncoordinated, people within this category may frequently be frustrated by their body and embarrassed by the lack of poise and polish that even the least coordinated of athletes possess.

In my advocacy experience with teens and adults, fewer people bring up sensory-based motor issues than, say, modulation issues. It's possible that many people with this category find ways to accommodate for the bulk of their sensory issues. They might just gravitate towards different sports, like running, which could mask some of the issues that come along with these particular challenges; joke about being excessively clumsy; or avoid complexities in movement altogether. Motor issues may also not be considered as problematic both to the person and within society, and so especially in adulthood, postural disorder and dyspraxia may continue to be overlooked by those who feel that they are "just clumsy." Still, there are others whose postural disorder or dyspraxia actually hold them back from living life to the fullest. When you feel as if your body is ineffective, it sometimes seems easier to just cancel dates and not pursue advances in employment.

Dysregulation

Dysregulation is the temporary state in which someone with sensory issues is unable to self-regulate (energize or relax) and maintain a calm, poised, and ready state. It's what happens when too much or too little sensory input is taken in by the differently wired system. And when the sensory system is *dysregulated* or *unbalanced*, all sorts of things happen. Whatever the sensory behavior is—whether it's craving, avoiding, ignoring, moving clumsily, or discriminating poorly—it becomes more pronounced and even more jumbled and complex. Dysregulated people with sensory issues may become suddenly polarized in their needs and behavior. It's especially possible for people with modulation issues to swing from one extreme to the other (like someone who normally craves smell might suddenly avoid smell). If a scale of typical behavior looks like this, with 1 being a very slow sloth after a few glasses of wine and 10 being a roadrunner on caffeine, most typical people fall somewhere around 5, that nice, balanced middle:

1	2	3	4	5	6	7	8	9	10

SLOWED DOWN BALANCED REVVED UP

With the right kinds of tools, treatment, and understanding, people with sensory issues can spend most of their waking hours within a notch or two of the middle. Without intervention, or if we overdo (or underdo) our exposure to sensory input, we may suddenly end up at a 1 or a 10. This is especially true for avoiders like me, who are almost electrified by sensory information. With the simple blast of a catchy song played a hair too loudly too late at night, we can jump from a comfortable-ish 6 to a fly-me-to-the-moon 10 in a matter of seconds. Someone with craving behaviors, on the other hand, might not feed their drive for input and drop from a 4 to a 1. Regardless of specific sensory issues, we tend to be all over the map when we're dysregulated—sluggish one second, overstimulated the next.

It's most important to remember that dysregulation doesn't happen in a vacuum. There's always a cause, as subtle as it may be to the untrained eye. It could be the smallest extra shard of sensory input or even a nanosecond without sensory input. It could be an ongoing onslaught of sensory information or hours without engagement. It's the straw that breaks the sensory camel's back (because that's a saying, right?).

Let's say a person with modulation issues—an avoider, on the whole—must put her sensitivities aside, wake up, put on some makeup, make conversation, have lunch, run errands, watch TV, and then finally at the end of a long day, spend the evening at a loud, busy, bustling wedding. Maybe she is feeling especially sluggish from not tending to her sensory needs during the day, but manages to slowly transition into the ceremony, feels a bit bolder at the cocktail hour, and takes the dance floor—bravely, I might add—during the party. Suddenly, she's mixing with the crowd, excitedly hopping on the dance floor, laughing, speaking over the din of diners and dancers. Still sensitive, surely, but bubbling, bubbly, and seemingly totally average and typical. She is Ms. AnyPartygoer, Ms. WeddingFunTime—maybe no one even notices her sensory issues. (As an aside, let me tell you, as an adult with SPD, some of my greatest social successes come from people having no clue that I even have sensory issues. It's like, *Check me out! A sensory woman hiding in plain view. If only you knew how complex my life really was, you'd name an institutional wing after me!* Just because the sensitivities are invisible doesn't mean they don't exist.)

What does our sensory superheroine look like as she crawls into bed hours later? What do you think you'll find the next day? My (supremely educated) guess is that she'd be a keyed-up, exhausted hot mess. She probably won't sleep because, having made the swing from somewhere low on the scale to somewhere high on the scale as quickly as her brain would let her to keep up with the energy of the evening, she is now pulsing with this energy. Tomorrow, once she can finally convince her heart to stop racing, her skin to stop crawling, and her brain to stop swirling around the events of the evening, she will probably crash again—something I call a *sensory hangover*. She'll need some extensive time to rest and regroup, to lift from the muck and the lethargy caused by the intense sensory processing challenges of the evening before, and to find her happy middle again. (This lift and related sensory hangover is less severe for adults with the right treatment, and might even be non-existent for kids in treatment.)

This rest and regrouping time during a sensory hangover is something I call *filling your sensory bank*, which is essentially understanding your particular sensory needs (especially after having been dysregulated) and going out of your way to accommodate them. If your system says, *"Hey person, I need darkness and quiet, and I need it now,"* it means using tricks, tools, exercises—whatever's in your arsenal—to slow down and respect the message your brain and body are sending to you. You know your bank is empty (and you've not filled it with enough of what it needs) when you end up at that polarized 10 or 1 and struggle to reach a nice, neutral middle.

So what happens when we've found our way to the outer limits? When we're incredibly overloaded by sensory information (something called, you guessed it, *sensory overload*)? When we're so lethargic that we cannot move or so wired that we cannot stop? If we don't work to refill our sensory banks and keep our systems happy, this dysregulation, when untended, often leads to two things: the two least-celebrated end-results of sensory issues, *meltdown* and *shutdown*. Even the words make me shudder. Nuclear plants have meltdowns. Governments have shutdowns. People with sensory issues have both meltdowns and shutdowns. We're Three Mile Island with a spicy political dipping sauce.

Meltdown

We've all seen a typical toddler throw a tantrum, and we're not so disillusioned when we spy a tiny tyke sprawled facedown across the avenue, clearly tired and upset. He has been pushed to his brink, unable to function for another single second, and we watch him kick and punch and bawl it out until he quiets down and inevitably collapses into a deep sleep.

This is not unlike a sensory meltdown, except that tantrums are often manipulative in nature while meltdowns are a necessary byproduct of living with a differently wired brain. I don't care if you're two or ninety-two, if you are a dysregulated sensory person whose particular sensory issues go unchecked for whatever reason, there's a good chance that the being who is facedown on the ground may be you. The meltdown may be triggered by a last-minute, surprising happening (a change in plans will do it for me) or even a source of sensory input that is just particularly bothersome. I can only describe it as a desperate darkness, a fearful and agitating cloud that casts a very black shadow over us for a short time and then leaves, but not before dumping torrential rain. It's not unlike a summer storm—quick to move in, furious in its depths of weather, and quick to move out. The tear-filled, anger-filled, upsetting episode doesn't last forever. Once the storm ends and the darkness fades, the sensory person will be left drained but better able to reconnect to himself and to the situation at hand.

Meltdown Etiquette:

Oh no! Someone you love is deep in the throes of a meltdown. What to do?! Scare them like they have the hiccups? Call 911? Summon a local shaman? Your best bet is to just give them some quiet space, see if they need anything, let them know that you care, and allow them to just ride out the storm. Never put them down for their outburst—especially teens and adults. They know that flinging themselves on the couch or on the floor or curling into a ball and sobbing heaving sobs isn't becoming, and so there's a good chance that they're already feeling really ashamed and silly. There will be no clarity during this episode, no time for them to realize how minor/simple/acceptable their trigger might be (it might actually not be acceptable within their reality, so don't expect a total 180 once they resurface), and no time for them to employ their tools, techniques, or tricks to help them cope. Once the storm ends, they'll come to in a daze and slowly regroup enough to evaluate the situation/input/problem with a keener eye. Are you the one melting down? I hear you, brothers and sisters. Cry your face off. Pound the pillow. Scream and kick. Hug your partner. I've been there, and I will be the last person to judge you. You will get through this episode, and I suspect things will look less overwhelming on the other side.

Shutdown

This is the darkest pit of the book, the bleakest section. It's the piece I wish I didn't have to write about. I say this because in my sensory life, my most vulnerable, raw, problematic moments have been shutdowns. The word itself makes me want to go hide. Give me your tired, your poor, your over-responsive masses—I'd even take the wretched, tearful refuse of a meltdown and the stigma from those who don't believe sensory issues exist. Just spare me a shutdown.

Someone out there is rolling her eyes right now, I'm sure. So much drama for such a clinical episode. To you, maybe—this is why I'm writing this guide. I understand much of the clinical, but what's cut-and-dry to one on the periphery is a tangle of upset to someone in the middle. Boo, you naysayer.

So what's a shutdown? So many conversations in the SPD community revolve around separating meltdowns from shutdowns. In my experience, a shutdown is like when a computer freezes and needs to reboot—except the computer is the brain, in this case. It's the end-all be-all of sensory-related attacks. It's as if the brain stops processing temporarily. It's an episode of detachment—much less severe for some—or an inability to connect to the sensory world and the people living in it, and it can last for a few moments or for hours. It's a fearful trip for others like me.

One moment, we may notice that things aren't feeling quite right. I know a shutdown is about to come on when there's a collapse in my functional visual field (as my brilliant optometrist friend would say, I process only visual details of places, people, and things, but not their wholes), and sounds become excruciating, as if the source of the sound lives deep within my brain and digs in even deeper with each honk or ding or hearty guffaw. Then the two lose their meaning and intersect, as if sounds become sights and sights become sounds.

I can sense (physically see and hear the difference in my sense organs), but inside, it feels as if I've lost all comprehension—I can't *perceive*. I can't figure out how to process sensory input properly, and I feel my brain working and struggling—like a tired laptop fan—until I lose my grasp on meaning. I know where I am, whom I'm with, what I'm doing, but otherwise, things become devoid and purposeless. This world holds nothing for me. It's then that my connection to the ground, to where my feet end and the universe begins, is cut. Typically unsure of my personal and physical boundaries, I completely lose the delineation and its meaning. This is often called *depersonalization* in psychology circles—feeling disconnected from yourself and your surroundings, or even *derealization*, feeling like the world is dreamlike and distant. Take it from me, it's terrifying to be present in one moment and then negated in another, relegated to a sphere in which you cannot make sense of anything and are therefore suddenly less present.

It's then that I become an anxious pod floating through space, unable to connect to sights and sounds and my body, and incapable of fully engaging with my environment. For all intents and purposes, it's as if I am blind and deaf and paralyzed. Sure, I am actually sensing—I'm a seeing, hearing, walking being—but I'm not processing or perceiving any of these things, and so, terrified and alone in spite of any present company, I blindly make my way back to somewhere safe, dark, and quiet where my senses can recover, my brain can reboot, and I can continue on with my day. If I'm with someone, I use him as someone might use a seeing-eye dog. I must rely entirely on him for the safe transport of my person. It's like I have a body and a brain, and normally they form some semblance of a unified front against the world, but during a shutdown the two detach from one another, and I am responsible for caring for them both—a creature consisting merely of thoughts dragging a body and a brain like Hefty sacks behind her.

It's not that I'm in danger, not really. Unless the attack happens as I'm parachuting or flying solo across the Atlantic like a modern-day Amelia Earhart (a time I'm calling "never"), I'm pretty safe. These shutdowns will not be the cause of my demise (and neither will they be the cause of your favorite sensory person's), but in the moment, unable to connect to the world, trapped within a brain that is malfunctioning and a body refusing to take directions, a shutdown feels like a tiny death.

Shutdown Etiquette:

Sensory teens and adults all have their own preferences when it comes to how they want to be helped during a shutdown, so be sure to ask them in a moment of clarity how you can best support them. The key here is knowing that you will remain a judgment-free zone, willing to bolster and not overwhelm the sensory person during this challenging episode. For me, this means reminding me that I am safe in spite of my inability to use some of my most crucial senses—both in words and in action. (I call my husband my handler, because in these most pivotal and problematic situations, he's not unlike a skilled lion-tamer coaxing his agitated charge to safety—and let me tell you, he's a natural Siegfried, or maybe even a Roy, since I'm known to bite when overwhelmed.) Many adults in the sensory community agree that deep pressure, in the form of handholding, weighted blankets, and bear hugs, also help calm their systems down. Are you the one shutting down? Know that you're not alone in what otherwise feels like very lonely (and externally imposed—surely not chosen) behavior. While you can't control the physical aspects of a shutdown or the nature of your brain's wiring, you can gear your thinking to be more positive in nature. I find that repeating the phrase "you are safe" during the earliest moments of a shutdown helps me remember that this is an episode, a time-restricted process that will inevitably end. Will you emerge exhausted and deterred? Probably. Will it happen again? Absolutely. Is it scary? Yup. Can it kill you? Nope. Will you continue living your best life afterward once it passes? Certainly.

Meltdowns and Shutdowns

In my sensory life, meltdowns and shutdowns are separate entities. I can't think of a time when one flowed directly into the next, although they've both been present over the course of a single day or evening and have ultimately stemmed from the same problematic source. Yet, I don't connect them. I think this is because, for me, the physiological manifestations of each—the heavy tears of one and the distant detachment of the other—feel so different. Crying is very grounding. In a meltdown, I am momentarily removed from the stressful situation and environment, but when I come to, I am damp from tears. I feel my body pressed against the solid floor. I am especially present. In a shutdown, I am the opposite of grounded. I can't begin to figure out where my body is in space, let alone the true parameters of the space. I feel lost, and I struggle through a fog of anxiety to make contact.

Meltdowns and shutdowns have some commonality across the SPD community, but as with everything related to sensory issues, our personal experiences vary enough to make each unique. For some, an unattended meltdown may well be the gateway to an especially brutal shutdown.

Time to Rhyme:

Because I'm a poet and I didn't even know it. I once tried to describe *meltdowns* and *shutdowns* to someone, and this is what happened:

A meltdown is anger and tears.
A shutdown is dissociation and fear.

A useful tip and a pretty ditty all in one. Snap, snap.

Transitions and Scheduling

Let's take a moment and think about the challenge of transitions. A *transition* is that moment in time when we finish one task or event and begin another. They're perhaps the most challenging activities known to sensory-issued people outside of being immersed in a tub of *[insert your sensory discomfort here]*. Someone with sensory issues doesn't merely end one task and begin another. We don't simply leave the supermarket and step out into the street—we change sensory environments. This is huge because not every sensory environment is a comfortable one. Some cater to our particular set of sensory needs, and some provoke our most raw and vulnerable sensitivities. We must readjust to the sensory environment each time we transition from one activity to the next, often stopping, stepping away, or employing a whole host of tools to help us settle in for our next challenge.

Because of the challenges we face in a transition, previously undiagnosed sensory teens and adults spend a good deal of time preoccupied with predicting and crafting the perfect series of activities to ensure their ultimate comfort and likelihood of success. This preoccupation makes the sensory person appear supremely rigid. The truth is, we are, and you would be, too. On the whole, we're a group especially interested in planning and scheduling. Setting up our expectations well in advance allows us to figure out how to best tackle the sensory challenges at hand. Our abilities might be stronger while sitting and watching a baseball game instead of playing laser tag (in this scenario, I have apparently somehow morphed into a twelve-year-old boy)—we're more comfortable with some activities over others, and will be better equipped to handle these events and their associated transitions if we can predict and anticipate our upcoming sensory atmospheres, requirements, and challenges. Transitions are still tricky, even when planned and scheduled, but at least our thoroughness helps alleviate some of the stress we're likely to encounter.

Let's Talk About Handlers

Part of the fun of being an advocate on the frontier of understanding is that I get to introduce otherwise-missing terminology to help the sensory community communicate more efficiently. This is how the term *handler* came into being. It's too long to say "The person who knows me and loves me unconditionally, who helps me function on a day-to-day basis, in spite of my sensory challenges, and who helps me face my inabilities as well as shows me the extent of my abilities." Yeah, phew. Hence *handler*. The term was developed for my husband, who serves as everything from my seeing-eye dog to my portable, human fidget. I love how the term has been accepted and used by the sensory community. Anyone can be a handler, as long as he or she is someone who supports a person with sensory issues and helps increase functionality and comfort. A sensory person of any age can benefit from having a handler or two in their lives.

Modulation Cheat Sheet

No chapter on sensory issues would be complete without this chart. What does each sense look like for every variation of modulation issues? Read each item like a sentence. For example, someone who craves sight will say "I crave ... bright lights."

Sense	I Crave . . . (Craving)	I Avoid . . . (Over-responsive)	I Ignore . . . (Under-responsive)
SIGHT	• Bright lights • Movement	• Bright lights • Flashing lights • Lighting changes	• Visual cues • Familiar sights • Gestures and expressions • Bumps in the road
HEARING	• Loud noises • Music	• Loud noises • Large groups • Crowds • Appliances	• Loud noises • Alarming sounds • My name • Someone speaking
TOUCH	• Touching others • Being touched • Balancing touch between sides of the body	• Unexpected touch • Light touch • Washing/water • Haircuts • Feeling messy or dirty	• Touch • Temperature • Being attacked • Wetness • Dirt • Pain
TASTE	• Intense flavors	• Mixing food • Trying new food • Brushing teeth	• Taste
SMELL	• Smelling objects • Smelling people	• Smells	• Offensive smells • Threatening smells

Sense	I Crave . . . (Craving)	I Avoid . . . (Over-responsive)	I Ignore . . . (Under-responsive)
PROPRIOCEPTION	• Textures • Chewing/sucking • Oral input • Purposeful crashing and bumping • Anything energetic • Weight applied to my body • Fitted clothing	• Mixing textures • Food temperature extremes • Hugging • Being moved by others • Sports	• Texture • My body in space • Posture • Position of my limbs
VESTIBULAR	• Moving my body • Moving my head • Rides/roller coasters • Being upside-down	• Body movements • Head movements • Rides/roller coasters • Heights • Elevators and escalators • Climbing stairs	• Moving my body • Moving my head • Heights • Being upside-down • Rides/roller coasters
INTEROCEPTION	• Excitement • Feeling hungry • Feeling thirsty • Feeling my full bladder • Feeling my pounding heartbeat	• Feeling hungry • Feeling thirsty • Feeling my full bladder • Feeling my pounding heartbeat • Excessive body heat	• Feeling hungry • Feeling thirsty • Feeling my full bladder • Feeling my pounding heartbeat • Changes in body heat

Chapter 5

The Neurological Traffic Jam

(or Senses Behaving Badly)

Studying Differently Wired Brains

What I'm about to tell you next is the most crucial take-away from this entire guidebook, in my opinion at least. If you feel like highlighting a single phrase, this would be the time to grab your markers:

In people with SPD, the brain is less structurally sound when it comes to sensory processing.

Despite critics' skepticism about the existence of sensory issues—most specifically SPD—Dr. Elysa Marco, a cognitive and behavioral child neurologist, and Dr. Pratik Mukherjee, a pediatric neuroradiologist, with their postdoctoral fellow Dr. Julia Owen at UCSF Benioff Children's Hospital San Francisco, performed a crucial, groundbreaking study published in the online journal *NeuroImage: Clinical* in 2013, in which they found *a structural, biological basis for SPD.* This makes Dr. Marco—or as I call her, Elysa (hi there, friend!)—one of my most favorite human beings on the planet and one of the most pivotal figures on the sensory frontier.

This study is the first of its kind, and is officially called "Abnormal White Matter Microstructure in Children with Sensory Processing Disorders." (It's OK, I was lost at first too. This is a fancy, science-y way of saying something like "Different Brain Structure in Children with SPD.") This study used an advanced form of MRI called *Diffusion Tensor Imaging* (DTI), a special scan used to measure the movement of water molecules in the brain, to learn about how brain cells, called *neurons,* physically connect with each other. The neurons have two parts: the *cell bodies,* which are generally found at the edge of the brain, and the cell arms called *axons,* which reach out to talk to other neurons in other parts of the brain (sometimes right next door but often on the other side of the brain entirely). The axons are coated with a fatty substance called *myelin,* which is white. Because of this, the connecting areas of the brain are often called *white matter.* The areas with the cell bodies don't have myelin and look grey. Can you guess what they're called? Yes, it's *grey matter.* So clever!

An excellent blog post on BioMed Central by James Balm calls white matter the subway of the brain. It connects the grey matter, which are the parts of the brain that do the processing—like that of sensory information. Different areas of the brain need to work together for us to do things like think, perceive, and learn, and the white matter helps with this. In typical brains, this movement of information from the back part of the brain (the sensory receiving areas) to areas related to integration (processing information from multiple senses at once), planning, and action happens unimpeded.

The group conducted this first study on boys aged 8–12 years, both with and without SPD as defined by the team's questionnaire. (A study on girls is underway, so hooray, this book will need updating sooner than we think!) What the researchers found is that these white matter tracts, the subway system connecting the regions of the brain, are different in brains with SPD versus brains without SPD. In SPD brains, white matter is in fact *less well connected* in some areas where we'd expect to see it, particularly in the back of the brain. Because white matter is responsible for connecting areas of the brain used in processing sensory information, we can say that people with SPD have brains that perform differently when it comes to sensory processing. This means that for people whose brains are wired this way, sensation—especially from multiple senses at once—and perception do not always happen quickly or even accurately. This makes the processing of sensory information difficult and at times even impossible simply due to the way our brains are structured.

Another amazing study from the UCSF Benioff Children's Hospital team—called "Autism and Sensory Processing Disorders: Shared White Matter Disruption in Sensory Pathways but Divergent Connectivity in Social-Emotional Pathways" (what a title), published in the journal *PLOS One*—shows that, while SPD and ASD share some sensory similarities within the structure of the brain, they also have critical differences. The first is that, in people with SPD who are not on the spectrum (meaning people with just SPD and no ASD), there is, in some cases, a greater disconnection in the sensory areas of white matter than in some people with an ASD. This may mean that sensory processing is indeed more difficult for people with SPD than with an ASD, especially when it comes to the processing of sight, sound, and touch. The team also found that, in people with an ASD, there is a difference in the areas of the brain related to facial emotion processing and language, but less so for people with SPD. This means that people with SPD do not necessarily have issues with these sorts of tasks. (For more information on SPD versus ASD, stick around and read Chapter 8.)

The SPD Scientific Working Group and the Sensory Integration Research Collaborative:

The Sensory Processing Disorder Foundation, founded by the phenomenal Dr. Lucy Jane Miller, is the leading organization in SPD advocacy, education, and research. The Foundation has gathered together and funded scientists and researchers from across the globe, including Dr. Marco and her team, to find research-based answers to questions about SPD, such as "What are the underlying mechanisms of SPD?" and "What are the genetic causes of SPD?" Answering these pivotal questions through research will hopefully change the way in which SPD is seen and understood by the scientific and medical communities as well as how people with SPD are treated within our society.

Structural differences. A biological basis. Distinction between two disorders. Wow. Now you see why I hold Dr. Marco and her team in such high regard. In an atmosphere of skepticism, and in an age where it seems ridiculous to dismiss what you cannot see with the naked eye without exploring deeper first—here are the first nuggets of proof that what people with sensory issues experience are not just figments of our imagination. I speak on behalf of my beloved community of delayed-diagnosis SPD adults when I say that this is the biggest relief. Having been dismissed by family, educators, and health professionals for describing our processing difficulties and having been misdiagnosed as only having mental health issues for decades, we can now point to physical proof that brains like ours are simply wired in an unusual way. Seeing this proof is like being given permission to exist exactly as we are for the very first time. We no longer have to defend the way that we perceive the sensory world because science steps in and delivers the much-needed proof on our behalf.

Other Studies

I'm clearly partial to one team's ongoing work—mostly because their findings are so supremely pivotal. However, a few other interesting studies on sensory processing issues are worth knowing about to help round out your understanding, and new studies are being completed every day. It's always wise to keep in mind that all studies have their limitations; these studies, however, show an important trend in the medical field toward studying sensory issues.

Davies and Gavin EEG Study, 2007

This study aimed to validate SPD, specifically related to how we *habituate* to sensory stimuli. *Habituation* is a process in which we stop noticing a stimulus—like a sound or flash of light—after being exposed to it over and over again. Let's say that a car alarm is going off outside. Honk. Honk. Honk. You may notice the first few honks, but if you're typically wired, you probably stop paying attention at some point. You become habituated to the sound, and this is how most people deal with sensory input.

In their study, Davies and Gavin looked to see how brains with SPD deal with the process of habituation through the use of an *electroencephalogram* (or EEG), a test that detects electrical activity in the brain. They found that, while typical brains without SPD, often called *neurotypical* by people in the sensory field, habituate to a noise or stimuli of some kind, meaning that they stop paying attention to it shortly after it starts, people with SPD never really do. It's as if the sensory input is new each time it occurs. No wonder people with sensory issues are often thought to have attention-related disorders, like Attention Deficit/Hyperactivity Disorder (ADHD). They describe feeling "startled" and "bothered" by sensory input. It's as if every flash of light, burst of noise, and subtle touch is new every single time. Once again, it's also another example of measurable differences between the SPD brain and non-SPD brain, lending more and more credence to the idea that SPD is a real, structurally based condition.

Parasympathetic Functions Study, 2010

Another study was conducted in 2010 by Dr. Roseann C. Schaaf and her colleagues at Thomas Jefferson University in Philadelphia, Penn., called "Parasympathetic Functions in Children with Sensory Processing Disorder" (published in *Frontiers in Integrative Neuroscience*). The study explored how the parasympathetic nervous system—a part of the autonomic nervous system, which is the area responsible for involuntary bodily functions like breathing, heartbeat, and digestion—is related to SPD. The parasympathetic nervous system's job is to help us recover from pain and stress—to take us from that moment of "ouch" or "oh no" and help us come back to our normal resting state of relaxation. The team specifically looked at how and if SPD children with *sensory modulation issues* (remember last chapter?) reach that resting, relaxed state after being exposed to sensory information. The participants also were rated on the Vineland Adaptive Behavior Scales II, a measure of everyday basic personal and social skills—from walking to preparing meals to cleaning the house to going to school—anything that you learn and can do to adapt to your surroundings.

The researchers found that the kids with SPD had low parasympathetic activity; their systems were never quite able to slow and relax entirely after engaging in sensory activity, while kids without SPD were generally able to do this just fine. The team also found that the kids with SPD scored lower on the measure of everyday skills. This makes sense. If you have trouble slowing down, relaxing, and renewing because of your system's wiring, you'd probably be more preoccupied by your inability to relax as well as exhausted from your efforts and have more trouble with—and less energy and patience for—basic tasks and communication.

A Note about Neurotypicals:

There's some controversy over using the term "neurotypical" to describe our typically wired friends. Some feel that it's derogatory, delineating one group from another by pointing out us versus them, while others think that we all exist on a sensory spectrum, and so we should not even bother making such a distinction. As an adult with SPD as well as an advocate, I find it especially helpful to use the term "neurotypical" when comparing someone with sensory issues to someone without. There are important differences in our wiring—neither good nor bad, just present—and so when discussing someone with SPD and someone without SPD, the term is used illustratively. It's the same as saying, "that person without SPD or an ASD," or "that person with more traditional neurology" and it fits in a neat, purely descriptive, judgmental-free package. In my opinion, we're often quick to tippy-toe around groups other than us in this politically charged day and age in which we live. I married a neurotypical, I was born to neurotypicals, and some of my dearest friends have not one iota of a single sensory issue. Sometimes, a word is just a word. It's our responsibility as a global community to assign proper meaning.

A Note about Studies on Adults with Sensory Issues:

You may see a trend here in the studies on SPD that I've presented: all kids, no adults. To my knowledge, there are very few significant studies on SPD focused on adults, and some—like one about sensory responsivity, anxiety, and occupational performance by The Spiral Foundation—are in process. Why are there fewer studies about adults with sensory issues? Well, children are often most funded in these studies. With children, we can see a purer form of SPD—certainly less impacted by social and interpersonal factors. (Kids don't yet feel the extent of isolation, fear, and anger that undiagnosed adults and teens with SPD often have, because they're typically in an environment of acceptance from an earlier age.) Because young children's neurology is also more flexible than that of their older cohort, researchers can see what works and what doesn't to correct sensory processing issues early on. We delayed-diagnosis sensory adults are bound to be studied in depth eventually, and until then we need to rely on the studies about children to help us understand our world. They're ultimately no less valid. After all, sensory adults were once sensory kids, too.

The Sensory Apple and the Sensory Tree

What about genetics? Let me tell you, this is nearly everyone's first question about sensory issues. I know many adults with SPD who only uncovered their own sensory issues after poring over checklists with their little one at an occupational therapist's office and realizing that their own challenges were, in fact, more than just quirks. Most SPD adults can also tell stories of their cousin who shrinks from light or their sensitive sibling. Although no genetic studies have been completed on SPD just yet, researchers at UCSF Benioff Children's Hospital San Francisco hope to finish some in the next few years. My smart money is on these studies revealing a genetic connection.

The Neurological Traffic Jam

No guide about sensory issues would be complete without mentioning the work of the pioneering occupational therapist and developmental psychologist, Dr. Anna Jean Ayres (called "A. Jean Ayres" in sensory circles). To her goes the credit for the name *sensory integration dysfunction*, which is what SPD was originally called, and the theory behind the condition, as well as the related assessment tools and treatment methods. Dr. Ayres is said to have experienced sensory issues herself throughout her life, and when witnessing the sensitivities of her patients, she concluded that the cause of their issues was related to the inefficient organization of sensory information in the nervous system.

Her work came about in the 1960s and 1970s, decades before the scientific studies I've already mentioned, and long before anyone started considering sensory issues. Think about the climate at the time. In the late 1960s, the American Psychiatric Association's Diagnostic and Statistical Manual of Mental Disorders (the familiar DSM) was only in its second iteration, and the since-changed diagnoses included everything from homosexuality (WRONG-O!) to autism as a part of childhood schizophrenia (NOPE!). *Neuroimaging*, or the specialty in charge of producing images of the brain, didn't begin to blossom until the 1970s. It's no surprise that we consider Dr. Ayres to be such a trailblazer in this field. At a time when so much of what we consider to be common knowledge had not yet been conceived or was completely incorrect, surely studying sensory issues was a radical choice. We're *still* struggling to get people to accept the existence of SPD in our current day and age, so imagine how it was for Dr. Ayres half a century ago.

Dr. Ayres laid the crucial groundwork for research on sensory issues as well as the methods used by occupational therapists to support people with SPD. She equated SPD with a "traffic jam" in the brain—the truest and most concise description I've heard to date.

Chapter 6 ✦

Sensory Issues across the Lifespan

Sorry, friends. SPD is not a childhood disorder, and sensory issues don't discriminate by age. It may seem that kids are mostly at the mercy of sensory concerns, but this is untrue. What we're really seeing is deep advocacy and some research funding for children with sensory issues at a time when these issues are better understood then they've been in the past. Between advances in science and the more recent spotlight on ASD, our society at large is suddenly becoming aware of sensory issues—especially SPD—for the first time. This means that the identification, evaluation, and treatment of sensory issues are more common and more likely, and so we're seeing many sensitive children on an earlier corrective path because their parents are catching their issues sooner.

This makes me sound about 100 years old, but when I was little (and walked five miles uphill and barefoot in the snow to school, clearly), I didn't know a single person who had SPD or an ASD. Neurological concerns, unless particularly challenging or especially pronounced, weren't identified the way that they are now. If they were identified, they were typically misidentified. Adults in the sensory community were called "picky," "spoiled," and "sensitive" as kids and were frequently misdiagnosed with a whole host of psychological disorders (more on this in the next chapter). This means that many adults managed to make it far into adulthood before even learning about sensory issues for the very first time and making the connection. I was 27 and in graduate school the first time I learned about SPD, and I'm friendly with many people in their 50s and 60s who just recently learned about SPD. We assume that if we had been raised as kids in this current generation, we might also have had our sensory issues identified much sooner, but we weren't and we didn't. Instead, as a society, we must all accept the idea that adults have sensory issues, too. This means that teens have sensory issues, college-aged kids have sensory issues, and many parents and grandparents out there are also secretly tending to their sensory sensitivities.

Sensory issues are life-long and come with different challenges at different stages of life. I believe that challenges depend on three important factors:

1. Neurology, or *if and how the brain can rewire*
2. Past history, or *whether or not negative social and emotional patterns have been established*
3. Phase of life and related environment, or *the extent and complexities of a person's roles and responsibilities during his or her current phase of life*

Childhood

As I mentioned earlier, childhood is the focal point of much of SPD's attention these days. This is a fantastic thing for many reasons. When sensory issues are caught early, kids can be guided through a series of exercises and use prescribed tools to help their brains significantly rewire. This rewiring potential is called *neuroplasticity.* The brain can create new *neural pathways,* or connecting nerve cells, to adapt to a given situation. When you repeat an exercise over and over, the brain begins to focus and develops new pathways to help you meet the demands of the new activity. This plasticity may be why people assume that children just grow out of sensory issues as they grow up and why SPD is affiliated so strongly with childhood—many kids, when treated early, can carry very little sensory baggage with them into adulthood, and so it's most prominent for them in childhood.

The brain is fully developed around age 25, and although it's possible to make many new connections throughout our lives, neuroplasticity decreases as we get older. This may explain why previously undiagnosed sensory adults often struggle to make smaller gains.

Although this rewiring potential may be the most significant reason that children seem to make the most and quickest progress, other things are important to consider. When SPD is caught early in a person's life, fewer problematic social and emotional patterns will have been established. Sure, kids with unidentified sensory issues are necessarily going to be the target of some bullying and teasing. Their most comfortable behaviors don't perfectly align with the behaviors of others. (Think of a kid with sensory issues, especially before these concerns have been identified. Maybe she sits on the sidelines in the playground, avoids playdates, cries easily, pushes, bites.) There's just less time to build a rich, complex history of traumatic childish torture and torment when a kid's only had a few birthdays before her sensory issues are recognized.

There's also less time to establish her own negative thought patterns related to her differences and the way in which she is perceived by others. She hasn't had decades to speak poorly to herself, constantly wondering what's wrong with her and punishing herself in turn. If a family is seeking treatment for a child's sensory issues, there's likely to be a better understanding and hopefully acceptance within the child's home and also within the school environment as well, and early on, the child will pick up on the message that, in spite of any differences she detects within herself, she is ultimately a good and worthy human being. In childhood, less time for baggage means an easier time accepting who you are and how you approach the sensory world. A big yay.

Also, when we're young, we have minimal responsibilities and very few roles that we play. Typically, we're children and we're students. We go to school during the day, and we spend the night at home. We're daughters and sons, brothers and sisters. Sure, maybe we play baseball or maybe we take a social painting class, but they're offshoots of the school or home experience. It's in this environment that many children find themselves beginning to struggle with sensory sensitivities and related, compensatory shifts in their behavior. While sensory children may be challenged, they play very few roles and wear very few hats. Typically, they're not ultimately responsible for their wellbeing or basic needs, and so their ultimate job is to rewire under the protective eye of their parents, teachers, and professionals. They don't need to worry about things like treatment costs or advocacy quite so early, and accepting who they are at a basic level, when in a loving and supportive environment, will come naturally.

Although children's biological ability to rewire plays the biggest role in their successful relationship with SPD, I believe that having less exposure to a long history of external distress and internal negativity, as well as minimal pressure from their roles, also gives them a crucial leg-up on the way that they cope with sensory issues. By the time children reach adolescence, their sensory diagnosis will just be an integral part of who they are as a person, and so they'll have a much easier time accepting their differences as they move forward.

Adolescence

From time to time, I hear from concerned parents about what seems like a resurgence of sensory symptoms in their child during adolescence. These kids were often treated successfully for sensory issues in childhood. Parents worry that tools that once were game changers no longer work and confide in me about their fears. It's hard enough to accept that there's something going on with your child. It is even more of a struggle when so much time has gone by to think that you did not catch such an important part of your child's experience.

As a mid-1990s undiagnosed 14-year-old, my own sensory issues became especially pronounced in adolescence. Of course, we interpreted them at the time as anxiety symptoms. After years of struggling silently with what I'd later identify as sensory sensitivities, the surging anxiety surrounding my challenges—and my sudden awareness of being so different—stopped me in my tracks and captured everyone's attention.

Adolescence is the transitional time from childhood to adulthood. The host of hormonal changes is enough to turn even the most cool, calm, and confident non-sensory kid into a greasy, cranky, fragile heap of fiery emotions. Now imagine a 'tween—a normally extra-intuitive, extra-aware, extra-sensitive child—the bearer of sensory burdens, making the same shift. Even if it seemed that they'd been handling their issues pretty seamlessly since earlier in childhood, the change that adolescence brings is significant for people both within and without the sensory community.

I once asked Dr. Marco, the lead in the biological underpinnings study, about why adolescence is such a time of upheaval for a kid with sensory issues. She said, flat-out, "Hormones." We're not entirely sure why yet; more studies will need to be done, but doesn't it make sense? Speaking to the ladies now (squeamish hombres, feel free to skip a sentence or two), who of us hasn't felt like our tenuous hold on the sensory world was about to crumble during our menstrual periods, only to feel more grounded once the cycle ended? It's like this in adolescence too. It's one very, very long cycle.

Add to the hormonal surge the physical changes that come about in adolescence. Where there was once no hair, there is suddenly hair. Where there was once a pair of nice, dry armpits, there is now sweat. Where there was once the hunger for one bowl of pasta, now there's a need for two. Where there was once a flawless complexion, there's now a zit forest. Hungry, sweaty, hairy, and pimply, it's no wonder that a sensory teen will suddenly feel extra-sensitive. Anyone who's ever had even a stitch of interoceptive awareness would suddenly feel it tenfold. The person would be especially aware of the extra sweat (and perhaps menstrual fluids) as well as the need to eat. Also, during times of quick growth, like adolescence, proprioception is found to be impaired as well. As proprioception helps us understand where we end and the world begins, suddenly the changes in our body, which are complex enough, are accompanied by fewer feelings of connectivity to the self and to our environment.

Not only is our biology in flux, but also our sense of self, our goals, our responsibilities, our social spheres, our family lives, and our place within our cultures and religions are changing. We're suddenly attempting to form an identity—trying things to see what we like and dislike and identifying what can be incorporated into our lives moving forward. We're also striving to fit in and find our place as more mature children, siblings, students, and friends, and, for the first time, as romantic partners. We're trying to strike the balance between the need for independence and our necessary reliance on our families. In the midst of all this change, very few things are stable on the emotional and social fronts of our lives. Take the fact that our biology is in flux, add to it the changes across the less concrete and more conceptual areas of our lives, and it is no wonder that even the most grounded, early-diagnosed sensory kid would experience some resurgence of sensory symptoms.

I always tell worried parents that, just because symptoms tend to show up early in most people with sensory issues, they don't just completely disappear. In fact, we're challenged throughout our lives to continue coping with our sensory sensitivities through physical, emotional, and social changes, regardless of how much we've been able to rewire through early intervention and treatment. Shifts in hormones and responsibilities sometimes draw attention to our particular challenges and make activities of daily living, as well as the roles we play, suddenly particularly problematic, and new tools and techniques are helpful in putting us back on track.

What happens when a teen with sensory issues wasn't diagnosed in childhood? I've spoken to many adolescents who are equal parts aware of their challenges and unwilling or unable to discuss them with their parents. Reluctant to accept ownership alone, hesitant to share the depth of their inner sensory world for fear of punishment, and contending with such major changes, many undiagnosed sensory teens either hide their challenges and silently punish themselves for their inadequacies or waver between disclosure and concealment.

In terms of neuroplasticity, teens' brains are still actively developing, which means that they will have an easier time than adults making new neural connections. The problem is that more than a decade into their lives, previously undiagnosed sensory teens have to contend with some pretty serious negative social and emotional patterns. They might be very aware of their differences and try to unsuccessfully fend off negativity from others and themselves on a daily basis. Feelings of self-loathing, embarrassment, and inadequacy might be frequent. Their world is also getting progressively more complex and demanding, with new roles to play and responsibilities to take on, and they must try to keep up with the changes and what's expected of them by others.

It's especially complex to be a teenager with SPD, regardless of whether this period brings resurgence or the first dramatic clues to suggest that something has been ignored for too long.

Adulthood

I'm not going to sugarcoat this for you. A sensory adulthood is a difficult premise, especially when no evaluation or treatment for sensory issues took place beforehand. As someone diagnosed in her adulthood, I feel especially protective of my experiences and the experiences of my fellow sensory adults. These experiences, however flawed they may have been, are the cornerstones of what makes me a kind, compassionate, intelligent, witty person. To deny myself of them is to deny myself of ... well, myself.

A few times in my life as an advocate, I've come across people who are quick to discount the delayed-diagnosis adult experience, citing that we're just too "messed up" or "too far gone" to be helped or even to be worthy of being engaged on any level. Once again, after surviving a full childhood and adolescence without the luxury of understanding what exactly was going on inside, as well as without the comfort of external support, being taken down for something that was beyond our personal and even societal control is quite harsh.

I know of a few sensory adults of my generation or older who were diagnosed in childhood. Some of them function quite well in adulthood, given their history, and claim to only notice their sensory sensitivities when they're especially provoked. (Not even a sensory adult diagnosed young can sit under a strobe light for hours without having a single feeling about it.) They are not unlike the Javan Rhino, rare and beautiful to behold. Some struggle in the same way as later-diagnosed adults. I believe that much of this disparity has to do with the same three factors that I keep bringing up: neurology, past history, and phase of life and environment.

Adulthood is filled with responsibility. We wear many, many hats—from *employee* to *partner* to *parent*—and in order to live and thrive, we must take the reigns of some of the more challenging aspects of adult life. We're officially responsible for our own survival and the survival of whatever family units we've created or still share. If we want to eat, pay the bills, have meaningful and gainful employment, love and be loved, and create and sustain new life, we have no choice but to fulfill these responsibilities to the best of our ability.

Treatment in adulthood is also complicated. Having surpassed age 25, the ideal cut-off age for rewiring, delayed-diagnosis adults make smaller sensory gains when it comes to permanent, meaningful neurological changes. Add to this the typical lengthy, unfortunate, and challenging history of most sensory adults—which often includes teasing, sensory discomfort, self-loathing, mis-diagnosis, and the development of related psychological conditions—and it's no wonder that we now try to catch children showing the earliest signs of SPD as young as we can. It's like preemptively salting the sidewalks in winter—why postpone a helpful treatment until long after the blizzard has started?

Many parents with young sensory children ask me what their children's adulthood will look like, and I always think back to those Javanese Rhino early-caught SPD friends of mine. With the right types of treatment and extra support during transitional times, I can imagine that early-diagnosed sensory children will function quite well overall in their adulthood with only a few minor hiccups. Because sensory issues are being treated much more frequently now, these children constitute some of the earliest generations being more comprehensively treated. We'll know more as they roll through adolescence and head into adulthood. Only time will tell.

Responsibilities and Abilities Across the Lifespan

For people with sensory issues, while our responsibilities and roles dramatically increase over the course of our lives, our abilities don't always follow suit. I always think of this concept in terms of letters and symbols (it's almost like I can do math!). In childhood, we have fewer responsibilities, and we have yet to develop or fine-tune our abilities. We can say that, typically, our abilities are directly in proportion to our responsibilities:

$$\textbf{A} - \textbf{R}$$

(This line represents an even and direct exchange of abilities to responsibilities in childhood)

In adolescence, our responsibilities begin to expand. Where we once were fully dependent on our family unit, we're now starting to take some minimal responsibility for others and ourselves. We're also growing our abilities by developing new strategies and uncovering new strengths that help us tackle our increasing responsibilities. Taking care of the dog? Set up a strict walk and feeding routine between school and clubs. Have a learner's permit? Learn to be accountable for the family car. For teenagers without sensory issues (or without any conditions in general—I believe that this concept applies to challenges across the board), abilities are usually in proportion to responsibilities. (Able to drive the car? Then you're suddenly also responsible for its upkeep.) It takes more work at this phase to develop the abilities than to meet the more intense responsibilities. Although the relationship is still direct, the two are ultimately more distant.

$$A \text{———} R$$

(Once again, an even exchange of abilities to responsibilities, with a longer line to express the increased work involved.)

In teenagers with sensory issues, we may see an increase in responsibilities without a significant increase in abilities. After all, our abilities are consistently challenged when we're attempting to cope with a differently wired system, and although we're now being held accountable for new behaviors and advanced outcomes, we might not be able to meet these demands as successfully or at all. This means that our abilities are not in proportion to the demands of our responsibilities:

$$A < R$$

The less-than sign is the perfect visualization for this concept. On the left side of the symbol, the two arms come together—perhaps we're able to do a smaller percentage when compared to our non-sensory (and non-challenged) friends. On the right side, it's clear that the two arms of the sign stretch further apart—just because we're able to do a smaller percentage doesn't mean that we don't need to keep taking on new, expansive responsibilities with age.

In adulthood, a similar pattern follows. As responsibilities increase, typically wired people figure out how to juggle multiple roles and requirements. Because they've managed to accommodate multiplying responsibilities in previous stages of life, they're able to use these experiences as a sort of springboard or stepstool to help them expand their abilities. It may not be less challenging than in teenagehood, but these typical adults may be better equipped to take on new adulthood challenges.

$$A \text{———} R$$

(This line represents an even and direct but more extensive exchange of abilities to responsibilities in a typical adulthood.)

For sensory adults who may have struggled with the increase of responsibilities in teenagehood, they find that adulthood is extra challenging. Having not necessarily been able to match abilities with responsibilities in adolescence, adulthood ends up being the heaping-on of even more intense roles and requirements. Once again, abilities may not meet responsibilities. If we're having trouble processing sight, and we refuse to present a PowerPoint in front of a large crowd under fluorescent lights at a conference for work, we could be in hot water with our bosses. If we can't tolerate the screams of our newborn, who will keep the baby alive?

$$A < R$$

(The sign represents the reduced abilities and expanded responsibilities in a sensory adulthood.)

So what do we do with this information? We can use it to better understand people with sensory issues in all stages of life. It's not just about how we're wired and our potential to change our brain structure; it's also about what we must face as we move through this world during the course of a single lifetime.

A Note on Abilities:

I am the first person to proclaim the extent of what I can do as a delayed-diagnosis SPD adult. I am proud of every single one of my achievements—of my advanced degree and of my relationships with my amazing family—but I am also very well aware that my abilities, as strong as they are, cannot be compared to someone without any particular neurological challenges. When I get through an event that pushes my senses to the brink, I often celebrate this small achievement, because what seems small for most is actually quite big for me. When I mention the reduced abilities of adults with sensory issues, I am in no way downplaying the significance of what we're able to accomplish in spite of our challenges. Our abilities, regardless of how different they may be, are truly incredible.

Chapter 7 ❧

Sensory Issues & Mental Health

I've spent much time separating sensory issues from psychological issues in this book—mostly to help you, dear reader, really understand how neurological conditions are different from psychological conditions. Now I'm bringing mental health issues back into focus. This is due in part to my training as a mental health counselor, but it's also due to my personal experiences and my conversations with teens and adults in the sensory community.

Dr. Sharon Heller once told me that SPD frequently mimics mental health issues and is also often accompanied by mental health issues. This still rings true for me, for sure. Because even I assumed that my behaviors were intertwined with one particular anxiety disorder, I can see how easy it is to make this mistake—especially in our society, where we are quicker to point at mental health issues than at neurological issues, even though we still have so far to go in the understanding and acceptance of mental health concerns. In my lifetime, I have been under the care of four psychotherapists—three psychologists and one psychiatrist—with only the fourth one seeing beyond the haze of mental health issues and detecting something neurological. If SPD mimics other, more widely acceptable conditions, how are people like me who have been misdiagnosed for years supposed to tune into their real issues?

That's how it always felt, too, like my therapists and I were never quite identifying the real issues at play. It was as if, with each new counselor and psychotherapeutic technique, we were becoming very dedicated to pruning a weed without ever thinking to dig down to the root.

And yet during my mid-20s, I began throwing the term "sensory stuff" around to describe my struggles. It was as if, although I couldn't pinpoint it, and I was not necessarily encouraged to do so, I still had this inner voice saying, *"Well, yes, we're anxious, but about what and why?"*

Undiagnosed sensory issues are crafty little sneaks, and it is so very easy to misidentify them, especially when some secondary psychological conditions make them more complex. Let's take one young woman who had been diagnosed with anorexia, an eating disorder characterized by self-induced starvation and significant weight loss. When she first emailed me, we chatted about her relationship with eating food. She told me that she couldn't stand the texture of certain foods in her mouth or their taste, and she just never felt hungry. Where a mental health professional without knowledge of sensory issues might see an eating disorder, I see someone who avoids taste, dislikes the sensation of certain textures within her mouth, and fears feeling full. To make things more challenging, this woman described feeling anxious around mealtimes and depressed afterward, when she would sit and mull over her inability to eat like the rest of her family. It may look like a mental health issue on the outside, but that inside—that root—is firmly based in the sensory experience. With occupational therapy and psychotherapy, her anxiety surrounding the eating experience and related depression dissipated, and she was able to better tolerate the taste and texture of food without feeling sick.

Most previously undiagnosed sensory adults experience some kind of mental health issue during teenagehood and adulthood. I think of these issues as little signs bubbling to the surface, indicating that something more is actually going on, but I do believe that, in the face of unexplained difficulties, we're more prone to developing negative thought and behavior patterns and so are ultimately more likely to acquire one or more related psychological conditions.

In my experience, this is especially true for anxiety. In life before SPD diagnosis, when we're not quite sure what's happening within us and we're exposed to sensory information that we biologically can't process, we feel unwell and dysregulated (maybe we melt down or shut down). We can't quite put our finger on why we're struggling. People peek in at our lives and weigh in. *What's wrong?* they ask, sensing our distress and discomfort. Looking around at the scene, which usually appears to be benign to someone who isn't as sensitive—imagine a stereotypically fun place, like an amusement park or kitschy bar—they can't figure out why we're having such a severe reaction to what seems to be absolutely nothing. *You're making a big deal for no reason,* they conclude. *Just relax.* When we can't stop making that big deal or are unable to relax, we turn on ourselves and become harsh. Their question of

"What's wrong?" becomes *"What's wrong with me?"* We learn that certain places and experiences evoke certain unusual physical feelings (again, we have no clue about our differences in wiring at this point), and these feelings are often punishing, so we begin to fear these locations and activities. We shy away from those who say we're making a big deal, and we do our best to avoid our critical inner selves.

Delayed-diagnosis adults with sensory issues are often misdiagnosed with one or more of these psychological conditions, typically in teenagehood or as young adults. While some of these conditions mimic SPD, others simply accompany the delayed-diagnosis sensory adult as he moves through his life's journey, such as the following:

- Anxiety disorders
- Depression
- Bipolar disorder
- Personality disorders
- Post Traumatic Stress Disorder (PTSD)
- Seasonal Affective Disorder (SAD)
- Substance abuse
- Eating disorders
- Dissociative disorders (Depersonalization)
- Attention-Deficit/Hyperactivity Disorder (ADHD)

Anxiety Disorders

As I mentioned earlier, I believe that anxiety disorders in this case are related to patterns of thinking and behavior developed while undiagnosed and may even be a biological end product of our particular wiring. Patterns are very hard to break. Although treatment for sensory issues may lessen a person's anxiety, especially as individuals learn to be more accepting towards how their body and brain feel in the presence of sensory input, a generalized anxiety would most likely saturate many of their daily activities.

Depression

When you're depressed, you feel lonely and worthless and find no pleasure in daily activities. Think about it in terms of sensory issues. If someone wakes up alone, again, because she's unable to sustain a meaningful relationship thanks to her supreme sensitivities; if she looks in the mirror and only sees someone who's always tried to live a complete, meaningful life but has been beaten down by her challenges; if she has spent decades in retreat from many people, environments, and activities; and if she cannot feel comfortable in her own body, it makes sense that she'd feel depressed. You'd be depressed, too. I know some sensory adults who fall squarely in this category. Although sensory issues are the root cause, their depression continues to loom even after treatment. Like with anxiety, it's hard to break these patterns of thinking and feeling.

Bipolar Disorder

One of my most favorite psychology-to-sensory switches has to be Bipolar Disorder, which is characterized by extreme mood swings—from *mania*, which includes pressured speaking and a flight of ideas (think of an intense, speedy high) to *depression*, which is that low of diminished pleasure, loss of energy, and worthlessness. As I mentioned in Chapter 3, this looks almost exactly like dysregulation. Over- or under-stimulated and needing to be grounded, I myself have chattered a million miles one minute and then, completely overwhelmed and exhausted, have vacillated into a depressive, lethargic state the next. If someone is especially depressed in the ways in which I mention above and gets no treatment for sensory issues, he might seem to be bipolar—

agitated, inflamed, overly alert or especially wiped out, moving from pole to pole. It would be very easy to misdiagnose sensory issues as Bipolar Disorder, especially Bipolar II, a milder form of the disorder. With occupational therapy and psychotherapy, a sensory person would become much more regulated and would more likely keep to that stable, neutral middle more frequently. Unless pushed to the brink by an unplanned, especially intense (or under-intense) dysregulating event, it would seem that people misdiagnosed with Bipolar Disorder would no longer have these symptoms.

Personality Disorders

Personality disorders are a wide-ranging group of conditions that all stem from rigid thoughts and behaviors that are characteristic of the person's personality. From Borderline Personality Disorder's unstable moods, behavior, relationships, and sense of self to Obsessive Compulsive Personality Disorder's inflexible devotion to rules and order, it's no surprise that many people with sensory issues were first misdiagnosed with a personality disorder. Rigidity, inflexibility, and instability are characteristics of someone struggling to understand their sensory issues and make sense of a world that seems out of control.

Post Traumatic Stress Disorder (PTSD)

Post Traumatic Stress Disorder (PTSD) is a very popular topic among teens and adults with sensory issues. Trauma from an especially terrifying event can cause PTSD, and although it has some similar characteristics to SPD—especially the oppressive anxiety; the sound sensitivity; and the avoidance of certain places, people, and objects—I do think that some people with previously undiagnosed sensory issues could also be struggling with PTSD. The trauma might not be directly rooted in a sensory experience, but instead happens as the result of not understanding the self and one's unique needs. When we're unaware of our true depths, we might be more willing to go along with something or someone whom we also don't read properly. Ignoring the inner voice that says, *"Something is always different about me"* would not be that dissimilar to avoiding the voice that says, *"This doesn't feel right"*—because, really, most things feel wrong most of the time for people with undiagnosed sensory issues. Having trouble reading the self, others, situations—it's not too far of a reach. Not all traumatic events are within our control, of course, but if we're unaware of the source of our sensitivities, we are likely unable to counteract the intensity of our reactions regardless of the traumatic cause, and so we're especially raw and open when we experience all events, particularly traumatic ones.

Seasonal Affective Disorder (SAD)

Seasonal Affective Disorder (appropriately called SAD for short) is a mood disorder like depression. The difference is that it always hits during a certain time of the year, like clockwork. I think of SAD as another possible misdiagnosis, because people with sensory issues do experience different extreme feelings and sensory sensations during different seasons. Someone with interoceptive over-responsivity (those who avoid internal feelings from their organs) might be hyperaware of how a particular temperature extreme impacts his or her own body temperature. They might also feel more proprioceptively grounded (and more grounded in a tactile way) in certain weather. Feeling the crush of depression in winter could be someone with untreated sensory issues and special interoceptive sensitivity to the cold. Unable to function as well as they do in the warmer weather, they'd most likely withdraw from challenging sensory experiences and people and be forced to sustain a lonely, pleasureless existence until spring.

Substance Abuse

As much as I've always felt the need to avoid substances, as they make my sensory issues even worse, many people with undiagnosed sensory issues turn to drugs and alcohol to self-medicate. Once again unsure of what's causing their struggle, substances give them a much-needed escape. Depending on which sense is giving them issue and whether the person is looking for more or less sensory engagement, he may pick from a wide range of substances he's deemed helpful in supporting and maintaining a regulated state.

I believe that sensory people who frequently deal with the fearful detachment of extreme shutdowns are less likely to turn to substances, because when perception is always tenuous and constantly in jeopardy, we'll do whatever we can to keep a firm grasp on our surroundings and environment.

Eating Disorders

Much like the young woman in the example I gave at the start of this chapter, anorexia can be the direct result of a specific combination of undiagnosed sensory issues, namely avoiding taste, texture, and smell and seeking interoceptive input. This person will go out of her way to experience no tastes or textures in her mouth, and she will feel most comfortable when she's hungry and her stomach is empty.

Binge eating can be explained by someone who craves taste, smell, and proprioceptive input and looks to avoid the hunger she feels thanks to interoception. Chewing will be grounding for her, as will the sensation of feeling full. She will be eager to always engage in the eating experience as well as to avoid feeling hungry.

Dissociative Disorders

Dissociative disorders impact a person's typical state of awareness, identity, memory, and consciousness. As I mentioned earlier, derealization is feeling as if the world is dreamlike and distant, and depersonalization is feeling disconnected from yourself and your surroundings, and both are experienced in different ways in dissociative disorders. These are very common experiences for people with sensory issues when we're overloaded with sensory information. It's as if the brain says, *Okay, thanks, but I can't take in another single second of input,* and stops processing, so the person feels detached from the self and the environment. Dissociation happens especially during shutdowns, and while it's terrifying for many, I've heard from a few people who find it comforting to be relieved of engaging completely, if even just for a few minutes.

Attention-Deficit/Hyperactivity Disorder (ADHD)

Seemingly as common as anxiety and depression for sensory people, ADHD is one of those pre-SPD diagnoses often discussed within the community. Hyperactive, impulsive, and frequently distracted, someone with ADHD can look much like someone with sensory issues. For a sensory person, when the input from a sense is typically so overwhelming that it's all someone can focus on, or when input is typically so underwhelming that she is always looking around for her next satisfying surge from the senses, she would appear distracted. And let me tell you, we are distracted because processing an environment while having sensory issues is very distracting. Take me (yet again!) as an example. I have intense auditory and visual sensitivities. I avoid input from these senses, because when I'm especially exposed, I must focus very intensely on sorting out, say, the conversation I'm having from other conversations and sounds within the room. The effort it takes to separate my conversation from the other sounds (to which I never habituate, if you remember the study I mentioned earlier) and respond appropriately means that I might miss something else entirely, like that I am holding my cup too loosely and am likely to drop it on the floor. From the outside, I look like I am overly focusing on one thing (I usually squint my eyes when listening, which is funny because it's often not about sight), but if you read my physical behaviors, like the dropping of a cup, I appear to be a bit unaware of my environment. In reality, it's the opposite—I am so over-aware of what's going on around me that I sometimes miss other areas of my environment completely, and I am especially oblivious to my own body.

The similarities between SPD and ADHD would be especially prominent when a sensory person is dysregulated. Someone who is dysregulated might for a time appear in motion or particularly chatty as he forces himself to find a neutral state of being. People with ADHD are also described as energy-filled beings who cannot wait patiently and who are always on the go. People with sensory issues are also frequently *fidgeting* or engaging the sensory system to either calm or energize by playing with a particular toy (more on this in Chapter 7), especially when we're feeling dysregulated. People with ADHD also fidget, bounce, and squirm when forced to sit still for too long. And let's also not forget the plight of the under-responsive sensory people, whose ignoring of sensory input would make them appear especially inattentive—again, not unlike their ADHD pals.

So how do we discern between SPD and ADHD? There's some debate about this in the sensory community. I've read that people with SPD will respond to occupational therapeutic tools and techniques (I'll cover some of these in Chapter 7), while people with ADHD won't, but this isn't necessarily true. A 2005 study by Dr. Kristie Koenig and Dr. Moya Kinnealey out of Temple University suggests that sensory intervention, including deep pressure and strenuous exercise, can improve impulsivity and hyperactivity in children with ADHD. I've also read that, when people with SPD are put on medications meant for ADHD, their sensory-based attention issues don't improve. To complicate matters even further, it's also possible for someone with SPD to have ADHD as well—the two are not mutually exclusive.

SPD and ADHD are separate conditions that sometimes exist together and can frequently be mistaken for one another. Sorting out which is which can be especially challenging, and for the person living with one or both conditions, it is particularly confusing. It may take treating the symptoms of one to help clarify if this is indeed the true, underlying issue.

Is it Sensory Issues or Mental Health?

Mental health professionals often ask me how we can begin to identify sensory issues in treatment. This is a wonderful question, especially given that SPD is currently missing from the latest iteration of the mental health Bible, the Diagnostic and Statistical Manual of Mental Disorders, or the DSM-5 (although I have faith that, with the new studies being conducted about SPD's biology and genetics, this will change in the near future). I always suggest that if a psychotherapist knows about and suspects sensory issues, she engages her clients in related lines of questioning. If someone describes his anxieties and they always stem back to small, echoey spaces, ask him about noise. How does he feel in the presence of the echoes? Ask about other senses, because the truth is that most people with sensory issues tend to have more than just one sensory concern. Does he find input from some senses to be more pleasurable? You may find that what was a clear and simple DSM diagnosis turns into something sensory-related, and based much more on what pockets of information you're able to access. People with undetected sensory issues have typically been put down for years, and their particular sensory concerns have gone overlooked, so they might be hesitant to bring them up to you and face professional scrutiny. If you lead the way, they should feel more comfortable and will be more likely to work with you to put the pieces together.

Is It Sensory or Am I Going Crazy:

I can't tell you how often people tell me that they think they're "going crazy" when they first notice their sensory symptoms, especially once they look past previously diagnosed mental health issues. It's tough. For years, it was as if those of us who went undiagnosed saw, heard, and experienced the world very unusually—unlike anyone else in the room. When we burst into tears after a loud and invasive sound took us by surprise, felt the need to stare at the brightest light, or walked straight into our armchair for the thousandth time, we were usually the only one having such a major reaction. It's like feeling an earthquake that only we alone experience. Clutching a doorway as the room sways, amazed that we're experiencing something so notewor-thy, we look at those around us and realize that they've not detected a single thing worth their extra attention. It's hard not to think that you're losing a grasp on reality when reality, the way that you interpret your world, is so at odds with how it's being interpreted by others. You're not losing your marbles. Your sensory symptoms are very real. Your world is as bright, loud, off balance, and in motion (or whatever your particular cocktail of sensory issues is) as you perceive it to be. It's okay to own this.

Chapter 8

Treatment, Tools & Techniques

Realizing you have sensory sensitivities may just be the first step, but it's the most important part of the process. Crossing the bridge from being an unaware, uniquely challenged individual to someone who is informed is huge, and the impact of this simple realization—this *Eureka!* moment—is absolutely life changing. Once you know this fact about yourself and once you've attached the proper terminology to your daily life-long challenges, you can't *un-know* this information. Instead, you are typically left with this sense that something more needs to be done. There's a drive to put this crucial information somewhere, to make progress, to connect with others.

Where do you go—or where do you send someone that you love—when you realize that your sensory experiences can be improved? And what can you do on your own to improve how you cope with your sensory self on a daily basis? As with everything in life, you have to *want* to feel better to see even the smallest of changes. The methods I list in this chapter take time and focus. Evaluations won't come to you. Changing your outlook won't happen without your willingness to make adjustments. You can lead a sensory person to water, but you can't make him drink.

For me, the crucial combination of treatment, tools, and techniques puts me in control of a condition that sometimes leaves me feeling powerless. No, I can't suddenly stop having SPD, but I can reach into my theoretical arsenal and pull something out—be it a physical item or a concept—and use it to make myself more comfortable in a given situation. Even for delayed-diagnosis sensory adults like me, life can improve drastically with the right combination of therapies, tools, and processes in place.

Some of these suggestions will work well for you, and some won't work as well. Age and experiences, as well as sensory needs and subtypes, play a key role in how we respond to different approaches. As much as I wouldn't feel comfortable at my age toting around a weighted stuffed animal in public, a young child would not understand the complexities involved in disputing an irrational thought—and as much as I would go out of my way to shield my overly sensitive ears to a wide range of sounds, a seeker might feel best in an auditory crossfire. You'll never know what works for your particular set of circumstances until you try different combinations.

Treatment

Occupational Therapy

This is the classic go-to of sensory treatment and is a fantastic place to begin a sensory journey at every age. Occupational therapists recognize that living is a job, and they support people as they operate as individuals within their environment. They help develop, improve, and restore independence for people living with various physical, mental, and neurological conditions in a very hands-on and practical manner, and the focus tends to be on *activities of daily living* (ADLs), or the basic ins and outs of someone's daily activities—like brushing teeth, cooking dinner, and working.

For people with SPD, occupational therapists, who are trained in Sensory Integration theory, typically take a *sensory integrative approach* to occupational therapy in which the patient participates in fun, physical exercises in a sensory-rich environment. The goal is for the patient to feel challenged and successful and ultimately to teach the brain how to respond more appropriately to sensory information. Some occupational therapists pair this therapy with other related therapies, like *listening therapy*, which uses sound patterns and frequencies to stimulate the auditory system and the brain, as well as the Wilbarger Deep Pressure and Proprioceptive Technique.

Another key aspect of occupational therapy is establishing a *sensory lifestyle* (or *sensory program*, *sensory buffet*, or *sensory diet*), an activity plan that keeps someone with sensory issues feeling focused, regulated, and balanced throughout the day. It can include any combination of therapies, tools, and techniques that I list here that a person finds especially soothing.

Psychotherapy

While occupational therapy is often enough for a child with sensory issues, I always also recommend *psychotherapy*, the treatment of mental conditions by talking with a psychologist, mental health counselor, or social worker, as an additional, equally important therapy for teens and adults with sensory issues, especially if their SPD diagnosis was delayed until after childhood. As a delayed-diagnosis sensory adult, let me tell you that nothing feels quite as amazing as finding a mental health professional that has not only heard of SPD, but also accepts and embraces your sensory diagnosis. My current psychologist was the first person to address my undiagnosed sensory issues, and it was her willingness to talk about SPD that ushered in this happier, healthier, more grounded phase of my life.

Growing up with undiagnosed sensory issues can be traumatic for a person, and many negative thought and behavior patterns are often established during these pivotal years. Psychotherapy is the perfect place to bring up concerns about the self, the past, life post-SPD-diagnosis, and fears related to sensory sensitivities in order to unravel some of the less helpful ways that we interact and react. Psychotherapy alone cannot change how we're wired in terms of our sensory issues, but it can have a major impact on how we operate within our world and how we integrate our sensory self with the rest of our being. It also helps us merge our childhood experiences with this new information in adulthood.

In my experience, both personally and professionally, I believe that Cognitive Behavioral Therapy (CBT) and Rational Emotive Behavior Therapy (REBT) are the two best forms of psychotherapy for people with sensory issues. During my time in private practice, I blended the two schools of thought with my own clients. I have colleagues who would say that no particular school of psychotherapy is best here, and ultimately I agree with them—whatever form of psychotherapy feels best will be best for you. If you can form a strong alliance with your psychotherapist, and if you believe that your work with her is helping you, you will undoubtedly improve, regardless of the techniques used. If you're starting from scratch and are not quite sure what type of psychotherapy to choose, I always recommend CBT and/or REBT.

CBT focuses on identifying, evaluating, and changing distressing thoughts and related behaviors. It's a very hands-on, problem-solving discipline that puts the patient in control of his treatment and gives him the tools he needs to succeed in making these changes. My absolute favorite CBT tool is *cognitive reframing*, which is the identification and disputing of an irrational thought based on a list of a dozen or so *cognitive distortions* or thinking errors, like overgeneralization (making a general conclusion based on a single occurrence of something), filtering (focusing on the negative and excluding any positive details), and polarized thinking (black and white/all-or-nothing thinking). We all think in these ways at one time or another.

Let's say that you are especially concerned about how you'll be perceived at an upcoming intense sensory event, like a party. You might think back to a time when you felt particularly ashamed to have sensory issues while at a party. Maybe you left the gathering in a moment you felt embarrassed, and you're afraid that this will happen to you again at this party. Using cognitive reframing, you'd be able to identify that you're making an error in thinking here, and you'd challenge your conclusions and replace your initial, faulty thoughts with new ones. In this case, you might think, *If I was embarrassed and ran away once, it doesn't mean that this will happen again. These are two different parties, and I might have a good time.* Cognitive reframing also urges us to ask the question, "What's the worst thing that can happen?" In this case, the worst thing that can happen is you will feel embarrassed again and potentially leave the party. You won't die, your family won't be harmed, and the people who actually matter will not love you any less (and if they do, clearly they're not people who matter after all).

Asking "What's the worst thing that can happen?" really brings clarity to an irrational pattern of thinking. When we're thinking irrationally, we're typically not in a situation that could cause us rational, real-world physical harm, and so this question is like a quick reminder that we will survive regardless of the situation, even if we are plunged deep into our worst shutdown to date. This is especially true when the faulty thinking is based on a previous incident. If we're thinking about past hurts, we've clearly survived up to the present, and so what didn't kill us then won't kill us now. I always think of this reframing technique as if I'm straightening a framed photo hanging on the wall. When you shift the image, you bring a clearer picture into view.

REBT is a strong form of psychotherapy that teaches people to identify, challenge, and replace their self-defeating beliefs and thoughts with healthier, more rational thoughts. In REBT, it is believed that we learn how to interpret our world through the lens of our families, culture, and past experiences, and our lenses are frequently distorted. It is also believed that certain activating events (like perhaps going into a shutdown or meltdown for someone with sensory issues) will trigger certain untrue beliefs about the self (*"I must act normally,"* *"I can't stand this for another second,"* *"This is awful,"* and *"I am such a broken, useless person"*), which lead to emotional consequences (like crying or feeling ashamed). None of these untrue beliefs are actually correct—there are no true, valid musts and shoulds and should nots in this world—and so our emotional consequences are also not always necessary. In REBT, a person will challenge her irrational beliefs and bring in new beliefs to replace the older, faulty thoughts, working to change how she interprets the happenings within her life.

Physical Therapy

I stumbled upon physical therapy by accident in my own sensory life, and now I recommend it to delayed-diagnosis sensory adults as another therapeutic option to help integrate some of the senses. In physical therapy, one or more sensory systems are very directly targeted and strengthened. I found a physical therapist who works exclusively with people with brain injuries and secondarily with people with sensory issues. Much as I did in occupational therapy, I participated in a battery of exercises involving balance and movement to help strengthen the interactions between the vestibular, proprioceptive, and visual systems. It interested me to see that the same techniques that improve vestibular, proprioceptive, and visual cues and the integration of these three interrelated systems for people with brain injuries also help people with sensory issues. I used to rock when I stood still, especially in the evening, and since starting my physical therapy two years ago, my need to rock has completely subsided. I am also better able to stand still and feel balanced without needing to lean on an object.

Optometric Vision Therapy

Under the care of an optometrist, vision therapy involves the use of optical tools, lenses, and prisms to help visual dysfunctions, processing difficulties, and integration issues. It can improve things like light sensitivity, dizziness, staring behavior, attention difficulties, balance, coordination, posture, and unstable peripheral vision, all of which are all too familiar to many people with sensory issues.

At first glance, people with sensory issues seem like less-likely candidates for this sort of therapy, mostly because they struggle with input from many different senses and not just sight, but much like a sensory friend of mine recently said, struggling less with visual processing means she's less likely to get so overloaded by her other senses. If you're carrying around a bag of bricks, removing even one brick from the bag will lighten your load. Much like physical therapy, vision therapy leaves fewer sensory bricks to tote around.

Tools

Don't break out your toolbox, we're not talking about hammers and slide rules here. Sensory tools are objects that help us meet our sensory needs by guarding against overwhelming sensory input (like sunglasses or tinted lenses, which help lessen visual input) or actively engaging the senses (like a trampoline, which promotes a stronger proprioceptive connection by working the joints of the leg). Tools are a key part of a sensory program and a necessary cornerstone of living a happy life with SPD. This is especially true for delayed-diagnosis sensory adults, who must rise to the occasion of many diverse scenarios while grappling with life-long sensitivities. We can't always rely on being in control of a sensory situation itself, and so tools allow us to meet our sensory needs better in spite of where we are and what we're facing.

The key to using sensory tools is being able to identify your own sensitivities, the properties of different objects, and how to combine the two. Once you understand what input leads to what sort of result (perhaps if you're over-responsive to sound, it makes you feel agitated), you can think of items that might help you counteract this input (anything that blocks the sound—I once even used a stretchy gym headband to cover my ears). Also, sometimes introducing better-tolerated input into the scenario may help, even if it targets a different sense. If you are over-responsive to sound but perpetually crave touch, like me, you may want to reach for a tool that plays to your desire for touch when faced with overwhelming sound. It's ultimately a more pleasant type of sensory input—you feel calm and happy when it's engaged—and so in a situation where you might feel inundated and especially bombarded, bringing in more positive sensory information of any kind should also help you counteract some of the other sense's problematic input.

If you have a creative eye and some sensory knowledge, you can look at the entire world around you as a market of tools to help you meet your sensory needs. A textured, heavy, door draft blocker could be multipurposed into a lap weight, which helps with proprioception. Earbuds can turn into earplugs if you're in an auditory sensitive pinch (maybe shut off your iPod, too). Tiny blue LED fairy lights can become a calming way to light a room all year round for people with visual sensitivities.

I am constantly identifying new tools or merging tools to meet the specific needs of whatever I'm experiencing in the moment. Years before I understood that my rampant anxiety had a sensory root, I developed an extensive collection of half-dollar-sized fur-trimmed and carved animal figurines that I'd tote around in the palm of my hand, always fidgeting without knowing what I was actually doing. I'd find gaps between furniture and the wall to wedge my body, hide away, and calm down. Delayed-diagnosis sensory adults often tell stories of the creative ways they met their needs decades before they understood what was going on inside. Plato famously said that necessity is the mother of invention, and I personally find that my early, creative years make seeing the sensory world as a toolbox now especially easy, because I learned at an early age to find the input that I needed in the world around me.

Less creative? No problem! Many commonly used sensory tools are at your disposal. Here are some of my favorite arsenal standards. They are by no means comprehensive, but they're the tools that I know the best because they're either pivotal to my own sensory wellbeing or they're frequently discussed within the adult community.

Wilbarger Deep Pressure Brush

Imagine an oval bar of creamy white complexion soap and add bristles to the bottom; this is exactly what a Wilbarger Deep Pressure Brush looks like. It was one of the first tools that I learned about in occupational therapy, and to this day it remains one of my personal favorites.

The brush is part of the *Wilbarger Deep Pressure and Proprioceptive Technique*, formerly the *Wilbarger Brushing Protocol*. Developed by occupational therapist and clinical psychologist Patricia Wilbarger, the woman who also coined the phrase *sensory diet*, this technique is a pre- scriptive method of helping the brain and the body calm and regroup through deep stimula- 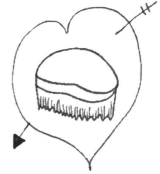 tion of the skin with the help of a Wilbarger Deep Pressure Brush, followed by compression of the joints. I am highly addicted to the process. I believe that the Wilbarger brush is one of the most powerful tools that exists for someone with sensory issues, although the technique is not substantiated by research, and many occupational therapists and other sensory professionals have reservations about the actual effectiveness of the process. I can only speak from my own experience, and I find the process to be calming and regulating.

The skin is our largest sense organ. This brushing technique not only engages the skin, but it also encourages us to connect to our proprioceptive sense, which helps us feel grounded in our body and in the world through joint compressions. It's also regulating because the process is scheduled for every one-and-a-half to two hours, so regardless of where you are and what you're doing, if you're using this tool, you'll have a very measurable pause to look forward to every few hours. What sensory person doesn't enjoy a nice, rigid schedule?

Even if you're not brushing, the scheduled pause is something that all sensory people should consider taking away from this brushing process. It's very easy to get ensconced in your work or play and to forget to take the time to regulate. Think of the brush every few hours and seek some quiet. Take a few deep breaths, reconnect with your body, and clear your mind—with love from your Wilbarger brush.

Fidgets

If I were somehow purposefully marooned on a deserted island (albeit a highly improbable scenario) and allowed in advance to bring one thing, I'd take a *fidget*. Fidgets are much as their name implies—little items that are meant to be fidgeted with, touched, stroked, twisted, smushed, and tossed between the fingertips. They usually have a special tactile composition as well as weight, movement, and pliability.

Fidgets represent one of those *necessity is the mother of invention* moments for me as an unaware and undiagnosed sensory kid. I could get away with buying and toting around little animal friends, because what little '80s girl wasn't dreaming of being a happy E.T. pressed into and hidden by a soft pile of stuffed bunnies and teddy bears? (Maybe it's just me, but that still sounds wonderful.) I quickly learned that the smaller the object, the more of them I could collect, and the less noticeable it would be if I cupped one in my palm to keep me company. I found it especially calming to have a little figurine with me while watching TV and am not ashamed to report that I still fidget with my tiny, childhood animal pals while hanging out on the couch with my husband. That's love, in case you're wondering.

Thinking about getting a fidget? Congratulations, your life is about to become awesome! You might want to consider something smooth and cold like hematite stones, a koosh or stress ball, putty, or even something faux-fur-trimmed. Anything that helps you focus and feel calm when you toss it between your fingertips can be a fidget. There are no rules. My only caveat for teens and adults with sensory issues is that you may need to learn to be extra creative, especially when you're outside of the home. It's hard to pass off a small toy as an adult, business-like thing to clutch in a meeting. I find that, in office settings, pens and pen caps are the perfect fidget items.

Either way, own your need to fidget and love whatever it is you fidget with that brings you peace. Amazing how a seemingly insignificant object can have so much regulating power.

A Note on Stimming:

When people with an ASD rock, flap, spin, or repeat words, this is called stimming. This form of self-regulation helps a person cope with anxiety, fear, anger, and intense sensory input. The nature of the behaviors, as well as their frequency, helps to determine what's "autistic stimming" versus what's just "traditional stimming" (like common nail-biting or twirling hair around a finger). People frequently ask me if adults with SPD also stim like our ASD pals. It's unclear and up for debate.

Personally, I don't consider fidgeting to be stimming, but I do it in the presence of intense sensory input. I also hum to myself, rub my fingertips across the palms of my hands when I'm especially overwhelmed (as well as my hands on my thighs), and before I started physical therapy for my vestibular and proprioceptive issues, I gently swayed when I stood still, especially at night. So what are these behaviors? Perhaps they're stimming, perhaps they're not—they don't necessarily fall within the bounds of traditional "autistic stimming." I'd like to say that it's OK not to have a perfect label on these particular actions. Regardless of their origin, they are calming and regulating, subtle and helpful. If you self-soothe somehow, that's just fine.

Earplugs

The name of the inventor of the earplug has been lost to time, but somewhere, he or she is smiling down at those of us with auditory sensitivities. I could praise earplugs from now until eternity. They allow me to sleep, enjoy weddings, and escape auditory overload when I'm on the go, and they fit right in the coin purse of a wallet. Plus, they come in different variations of Noise Reduction Ratings (the fancy NRR), measured in decibels or sound levels. Earplugs, in my opinion, are one of those near-perfect tools for sensory adjustment. They need to be shoved in the ear, which is their only downfall, and most of them degrade with each use, but they've pulled me from the brink of some very sticky (i.e., loud) situations.

People often ask me what I look for in an earplug. This is one of those cases where trial is key—buy a few brands of earplugs and try them out. Our tolerance levels surely vary as broadly as our sensory sensitivities. I'm partial to foam earplugs by Hearos. When I sleep, I prefer 33db plugs, and when I'm awake and need to function, I like the 32db ones. I once tried a generic store brand, and they left my auditory canal all sorts of colorful, so I tossed them. Unless you're excited about becoming the next modern art project, buyer beware.

Earmuffs

These auditory-reducing puppies are like a cross between the snuggly earmuffs of your childhood winters and vintage headphones on steroids.

I recently bought my first pair of earmuffs, which are essentially earplugs that cover the entire ear from the outside, and I'm a big fan. A sensory friend of mine loves her earmuffs, not only for their sound-reducing quality, but because they squeeze the sides of her head, which she finds super calming. Having used my *handler* for this same side-of-the-head-squishing-during-tense-moments many times before, I was thrilled to see that my earmuffs not only reduced sound, they made me go *"Ahhhh."* Thanks anyway, handler, I've got this one covered!

Earmuffs are a great alternative for "sensory sensitives" who can't tolerate the weird press of earplugs in their auditory canals. Although they're more obvious to others because they rest on the outside of the head and ears, they look so much like vintage headphones that they usually go unnoticed.

Noise-Canceling Headphones

These are the gold standard of auditory protection. On my wish list, after a trip to literally anywhere tropical, are noise-canceling headphones. The good ones are very costly and look pretty similar to earmuffs, but instead of reducing sound, these headphones are said to cancel sound. Ah, the sound of silence. Apparently there's a microphone in the headphones that picks up on *ambient noise*, or background noise. *Active* noise-canceling headphones cancel both high- and low-frequency sound waves, while the *passive* kind more frequently blocks high-frequency waves.

However they work, some of the best, most expensive (and therefore most technologically sound) pairs are lauded by the sensory community. If I can ever scrape together enough money to try a pair, I'll let you know what I think.

Tinted Glasses

When I was first evaluated for SPD, my occupational therapist heard what I had to say about my love of looking at the color blue and recommended that I check out tinted glasses. At a street fair, I boldly walked a few blocks through the chaos to find a sunglasses kiosk and picked out a large pair of dark-blue tinted aviators. They were less sunglasses and more quirky fashion statement, and they quickly transformed my face into a character in every 1970s buddy cop movie and TV show. I loved them instantly for how they let me see the world around me: smoother, less gritty, and less sharp. I noticed that I was more often than not better able to process the whole of an item or person and not just the details with the glasses on my face. However, at work and in graduate school, I felt like I looked insane. Strangers, classmates, and coworkers turned their heads as I passed by—because really, who wears sunglasses indoors—and such big, old-timey ones to boot? I was known as The Girl with the Blue Sunglasses. People asked me about them incessantly. I should've just worn a big button that said "Ask Me About My SPD."

Six months later, I went to see an optometrist who frequently works with people with brain injuries and sensory issues (I always muse how these two are paired together sometimes in the medical community—so different and yet so similar), and she told me all about the science behind my blue-tinted lenses. Lenses with any color tint prevent certain spectrums of light from reaching the eye. One theory on why blue is such a well-tolerated option is that blue light lessens the hyper-excitability of the brain in people with brain injuries and sensory issues, as well as cuts down on the quick and subtle flickering of fluorescent lighting detected by the same sensitive systems.

There are also two pathways in the brain: the *parvo* or "what" pathway, responsible for our seeing detail, and the *magno*, or "where" pathway, responsible for our seeing the periphery, detecting motion, and seeing the whole of objects and people. Both need to be balanced for a happy visual experience, but frequently for people with either brain injuries or sensory issues, the parvo is overstimulated and the magno is understimulated. This could easily explain why I am always fighting to see beyond every little detail to process the whole visual scene. The color blue is said to stimulate this magno pathway and restore balance. In short, these tinted glasses, especially in my chosen blue color, cut down on the visual sensory information that makes me feel uncomfortable and unwell. Since my brain has trouble doing this filtering, the glasses do it for me. Brilliant.

I highly recommend that all visually sensitive people find a pair of tinted glasses ASAP. Meet with an optometrist, especially one who's either heard of SPD or worked with brain injuries, and go for an evaluation. I was prescribed two blue tints of non-prescriptive glasses—one darker, one lighter—which I wear over my contacts when I'm outside or away from home (and sometimes at home if I am feeling particularly sensitive). See what works for you. These glasses have been life-changing for me. I can move further through this sensory world and sustain visual input longer, thanks to the fabulously nerdy, light blue glasses on my face.

Weighted Blanket

I don't have the best track record for sleep. I was never a completely poor sleeper, but there was always a list of items I'd need to check off before I'd be able to nod off. The room had to be cold and quiet. I had to have the right combination of sheets, blankets, and stuffed animals. Even then, I slept pressed up against the wall that flanked my bed. I always felt anxious before bed, aware that if things weren't just so, I'd be up darting back and forth from the bathroom all night—having interoceptive struggles long before I knew the proper terminology. Once I was put on anti-anxiety medication, I worried less about sleeping and rested well in the thought that, regardless of situation, the drug would knock me out cold.

My sleep life changed completely once I bought a weighted blanket, and if you struggle with proprioception issues, you might want to consider buying or making one. Nothing cramps a sleeping style like not knowing where your body is in space, especially when your eyes are shut. If you feel calmed by weight or tight squeezes, you will love owning a weighted blanket.

People who've never heard of weighted blankets laugh when I tell them that I sleep under 17 lbs, and it's a fun party trick to have someone pick up what looks like a nebulous blanket and find it to weigh as much as a seven-month-old. The formula for picking a weighted blanket's weight is 10% of your body weight plus one pound. If you gain a few pounds, you'll actually notice that the blanket feels lighter and less calming, and so it's a good motivator to keep your weight at bay. Weighted blankets are costly to buy and difficult to make, and so you'll want to avoid replacing yours. Also, consider the blanket's fabric. I ordered a chenille material, which my hungry fingertips love as I drift off to sleep, so it's like having a proprioceptive and tactile tool in one.

Best Weighted Blanket Formula:

10% of your body weight + 1 pound

Weighted Sleep Mask

If you're like me and can never have enough weight or pressure against your body, you'll also love sleeping with a weighted sleep mask. Another multipurpose tool, these masks are weighted for proprioceptive purposes and are sometimes filled with dried lavender, which could be an olfactory boon if you like the smell. They also block the light, which is key for those of us with visual sensitivities, and are lined with different fabrics—mine, once again, is chenille. At night, I am basically ensconced in weighted pink chenille. Hey, good-looking.

This is one of those tools that I didn't know existed until I needed it and did some research. One night, after a particularly taxing sensory day, I lay in bed fluttery and anxious and unable to slow down. My handler, ever creative, pushed his flat palm against my closed eyes and surrounding face, and I felt my entire body go limp. All racing thoughts ceased, and I was able to feel myself breathing deeply. After he removed his hand, I looked up at him, and he looked down at me, both of us surprised that such a simple gesture would have such a big impact on my wellbeing. These days, I refuse to sleep without my weighted sleep mask. My body likes knowing where it is in space—and guess what, so does my face.

Weighted Lap Pad

Although I am new to owning a real weighted lap pad, which is basically like a mini weighted blanket for your lap (perfect for daytime hours and activities, as well as travel), I've been sitting with weight on my lap—as well as on my chest—for a few years now. I've used a weighted scarf, a weighted ice pack, my laptop, my purse, any passing little kid—children are the best lap weights when they sit still—and now, I am finally using a proper lap pad. Once again, people with proprioceptive issues, especially those whose systems ignore input from this sense, will feel calmer and more connected when seated under a weighted lap pad.

Trampoline

Even as a little kid, I loved to jump. Watch any of my family's old home movies from when I was around four, and you'll see me bouncing in rapid succession across the screen with the widest smile plastered across my face. Of course I was smiling—jumping engages the knee joints and helps with proprioception, which, as we all know, is a very powerful and regulating sense.  At a time when my sensory issues were unclear and essentially in hiding, my body still looked for any opportunity to regulate. Jumping was ecstasy.

Years later, I am still a jumper, and I still can't help but smile as I propel myself into the air and crash back down to the ground. Back in 2010, I hunted down a mini exercise trampoline, and now it's a permanent fixture in our apartment. I love touring friends around our space, because when they come upon a random trampoline, they always ask if I teleported in from a bizarre 1980s exercise video and where I'm hiding my leg warmers. Of course, I always urge them to take a quick hop. (Interesting fact, very few people turn down a chance to jump on a trampoline.)

A portable trampoline is the perfect tool for someone with limited space who also dreams of living in a sensory gym.

Chewables

If provoked, I will bite you and any other meaty fingers that get in my way. It's not because I am a vampire or some unchained mutt (as far as you know), it is that I just often have the urge to sink my teeth into things—"often" meaning when I am inundated with sensory information. During private, meltdown-y moments, I have sunk my teeth into pillows, stuffed animals,

110

paperback books, and friendly and familiar arms. I am always looking to chew and crunch with every meal, and will actually not register having eaten if I don't toss some toothy foods in my mouth every few hours.

Oral input is very regulating for some of us, especially if we struggle with proprioception issues, and biting, chewing, and sucking are fabulous for the jaw joints and the various muscles around the mouth. Chewable objects exist out there in the form of jewelry and trinkets, but I find it even easier as an adult to chew things like gum, ice cubes, fruit leather, and pretzels—no one, regardless of his or her wiring, will look at you sideways if you pull out a stick of gum in a sensory moment.

Also consider the plastic straw—chewable, suckable, and socially friendly.

Smellables

Two words: essential oils.

Although I have no real sensory relationship with smells besides noticing them (I don't crave them, I don't avoid them, and I don't fail to notice them), I am a huge fan of essential oils for those times when I want to use smells to promote the way I feel. *Essential oils* are distilled, natural oils from parts of plants. As someone with anxiety issues, I am a lavender fanatic, and my tiny bottle of lavender essential oil scents my daily relaxing Epsom salt baths and my hand creams and dot my wrists, the soles of my feet, and the pulse points behind my ears each night. I also love peppermint essential oil, and I find this smell to be a focusing, centering scent for daytime that (bonus!) helps with nausea.

Overwhelmed by unfamiliar smells? Find a scent or two that are soothing to you and tote them around with you—take a whiff when other smells become an issue. Crave smells? Stop and smell the roses.

Herbal Tea

Can a drink be a tool? Who knows, but herbal tea is one of those insta-re-laxation tools in my arsenal. There's something about the weight of a mug in my hand and the repetitive motion of lifting mug to mouth that calms me down every time. I adore many things ice cold, but I love pushing my face against the steam rising from a cup of tea and momentarily losing myself in the heat. I usually turn to chamomile or chamomile-lavender (because there's clearly never enough lavender in my life). A drop of honey, and I am ready for sleep.

Techniques

Somewhere between the therapies and the tools are a handful of tech-niques that, in my humble opinion, make my sensory experience complete. Unlike therapy, you don't have to venture anywhere, and unlike tools, you don't have to tote anything around with you. All you need is yourself and maybe a little bit of guidance from me.

Humming

As I mentioned earlier, humming is one of those things I do when I need to reconnect to my body and the environment. As I'm less likely to carry around a fidget, when I'm on the go I will frequently turn to humming an up-beat, familiar song. Similarly, many people with SPD like to talk—and loudly! Perhaps the hum that happens within our throats and chest when we speak aloud is soothing for a reason.

It turns out that humming may have important roots in human evolution. Some scientists theorize that humming might have once served to let others know that we were okay and not in danger. (Go ahead, hum while being attacked by a pack of big cats, I'll wait.) Similarly, it's a subtle message to our-selves that we're okay, regardless of how we feel in our bodies in the sensory world, much like saying to ourselves, "you're safe," during a shutdown. Other scientists theorize that humming stimulates the vagus nerve, the cranial nerve that keeps the heart rate constant and controls digestion, sending out signals to reduce activity in the areas of the brain related to depression.

Deep Breathing

Deep breathing is especially amazing for us sensory folks who also have anxiety issues, and it is great for people who generally feel stressed. This simple technique increases the oxygen supply in your brain and invites a state of calm by triggering the parasympathetic nervous system (this process is typically challenging for people with SPD), as well as connects you with your body—all of which are fantastic when you live in a perpetually agitated fleshy sensory encasement.

Ready? Let's go.

Sit comfortably or lie down somewhere that is sensory friendly and close your eyes. Put your hands on your stomach. Inhale through your nose for a slow count of five and then exhale through your lips for a slow count of five. Feel your belly rise and fall under your hands, and try not to raise your chest. Continue to do this for the next few minutes. If you're feeling relaxed, you can change the count to eight or even ten.

Combine your deep breathing exercise with the next technique to really further your relaxation potential.

Visualization

My kingdom for visualization! I am a deep-breathing and visualization fanatic, and it's the final phase of my pre-sleep preparation every single night. Visualization is an amazing way to set a busy mind free. A beloved yoga instructor used to lead my class through a pre-session visualization, and she'd always have us imagine letting the day go like a parcel into the evening. My parcels of the day always floated away in the baskets of tiny imagined hot air balloons or were tossed like crates into the river. When you can envision letting things go in your mind's eye, it makes for a truly more grounding experience when you refocus back into reality.

If you have sensory issues, you may find yourself resisting this forced slow down at first. Your brain may still be racing, your body may feel detached, and even your ears may be ringing. This is okay. As you already know, our parasympathetic nervous systems are such that they're not good at regulating relaxation on their own. It is up to us to bring relaxation to our systems, which in turn helps us regulate our sensory input intake. Have patience with the process! ·

Find some sensory-friendly space. Sit or lie down in a comfortable position and close your eyes. You can start with a few deep breaths, as described above. Begin to imagine a safe place that agrees with your sensory needs. Is it the shoreline of your favorite beach? An imaginary castle situated at the top of a peaceful, green mountain? A field of dewy grass at twilight? The mosh pit of your favorite concert? Under the covers of your bed? In the arms of your partner or curled up with your favorite pet? In your mind's eye, notice the details. Do you hear the sound of crickets? Are gentle waves crashing? Is your cat purring? Do you feel the sand between your toes? Allow yourself to spend some time in this space, and feel free to continue deeply breathing as you visualize your presence in this location.

Hitting the Deck

Another one of those terms I've created because I had a practice and saw a need, I find that when I'm trapped in the most overwhelming sensory moments, nothing feels quite as right as *hitting the deck*, or sprawling out on the floor (be it wood or carpet) on my back with my legs and arms splayed like Da

Vinci's famed Vitruvian Man. By hitting the deck, someone with proprioceptive issues can press skin and joints against the solid ground, connecting his entire physical self to the still, strong earth. Many times, my need to hit the deck coincides with a meltdown, and I typically emerge from these moments feeling calm and refreshed.

Yoga Nidra

Lately, you can find me sprawled out on the floor for a half hour each day, deep in the throes of *yoga nidra*, or a conscious, sleep-like meditation exercise. I just love yoga nidra, which feels like a step up from hitting the deck with a dash of deep breathing and visualization. This is not your typical yoga. Yoga nidra can be done regardless of your physical ability, because it all happens as you lie perfectly still on your own floor or bed. No twisting or turning. If you can lie down, breathe, and use your imagination, you can do yoga nidra. (Just google "yoga nidra" and give one of the guided videos a whirl.)

In each yoga nidra session, you are invited to close your eyes, imagine the room and the environment outside, make peace with the immediate and distant sounds, and then visualize the presence of each part of your body and its presence in physical space—especially helpful for someone like me with proprioception issues. By imagining each body part in your mind and encouraging the part to relax, your body will ultimately release all tension and gradually melt into the ground. Some practitioners will then guide you through a series of peaceful images, like the setting sun, the golden ocean waves, a bonfire on the sand, and roses in bloom in a bountiful garden. I often find myself seeking visuals of these scenarios in my daily day to enhance my yoga nidra visualizations, sometimes challenging myself to push far beyond my initial neurologically based visual discomforts and find scenes in real life that correspond with this soothing, meditative practice.

Yoga nidra also takes a wonderful form. You're lead into the meditation with one set of words and guidelines, including the recognition of a goal or resolve related to your personal challenges, and you're lead back out with the same set of words and guidelines. It's like retracing your steps out of the friendly darkness and back into the sensory world. I always leave the practice feeling calm and centered, the vice of anxiety loosened from operating with my particular sensitivities.

Thought Stopping

Thought stopping is a behavioral technique that helps us to control our negative ideas through the simple tap of the wrist, flick of a rubber band around the wrist, or clap of the hands in the middle of an endless repeat of unhelpful thoughts. It can be useful for sensory people with anxiety issues, as it helps to stop cyclical and ongoing rumination, although many therapists no longer use this technique in their work. Some say that stopping negative thoughts only causes their re-emergence.

Personally, I find some thoughts so overwhelming—especially before a challenging sensory event or after a less-than-successful event—that I get truly ensconced in their swirl. I think them over and over and over until I have lost touch with reality and am singularly focused on how I handled myself, how I will handle myself, what people will say about me, how I felt in the moment, how I feel in the moment. When I realize that I am stuck in one of these whirlpool thoughts, thought stopping allows me to take a pause, step back from the thought, evaluate it, and pick a newer and more useful thought. It's like falling asleep underwater, waking up con-

fused, and swimming to the surface for air. The tap—actual or envisioned—catches a thought that is spinning around like a broken record and gently removes the disc. (Anyone else out there remember records? No? Okay.)

The Most Powerful Tools of All:

Acceptance and Accommodation—For delayed-diagnosis sensory adults, sometimes the most powerful tools in our arsenal are the simplest ones. Acceptance and accommodation, although nebulous in concept, have the potential to be life altering. We must learn to accept that, sometimes, regardless of what else we do, many decades of our lives passed before we understood our sensory needs and received a proper evaluation. We must learn to accept that we are differently wired, and therefore our needs are unique. Regardless of what happens, we have sensory issues, and that's okay. Our best bet is to accommodate our needs as well as we can, to be as candid with others about our challenges and our requirements for feeling more comfortable, and to be honest with ourselves about our needs. There's no shame in accommodation. In fact, I'd say that there's strength to be found in knowing exactly what you require to be the best version of yourself. You deserve to feel as well as possible on a daily basis, and you owe it to yourself to practice self-kindness.

Chapter 9

Sensory Issues in SPD & ASD

People often confuse SPD with *ASD*, the general term used for Autism Spectrum Disorders. SPD and ASD are not the same thing, even though they share some similarities. Some people have both SPD and ASD—in fact, according to The Sensory Processing Disorder Foundation, about 75% of children with an ASD have significant symptoms of SPD (Temple Grandin, the noted autistic author and speaker, has even said that everyone with an ASD has sensory issues), but most people who have SPD aren't on the spectrum and do not also have an ASD.

If we say that SPD is the same as an ASD, it's like saying that sorbet is ice cream. Both sorbet and ice cream are frozen treats. Both make amazing desserts, especially in the depths of the hottest summer. Both are scooped into bowls or cones. Both are tasty. However, ice cream is made with sweetened milk, and sorbet is made with sweetened water. They're ultimately similar—related but different. You can get the sense of one if you know about the other. I also like to think of SPD and ASD as cousins stemming from the same branch of a family tree—we are all members of the same sensory family, but our origins vary.

SPD and ASD:

Many people with an ASD have SPD, but most people with SPD don't have an ASD. SPD is not a disorder on the autism spectrum, even though most people on the autism spectrum have significant sensory symptoms.

If you have read this whole book and haven't just chapter-hopped (both are A-OK, by the way), you'll remember that, in Chapter 5, I brought up the study undertaken by my research pals at UCSF Benioff Children's Hospital San Francisco called, "Autism and Sensory Processing Disorders: Shared White Matter Disruption in Sensory Pathways but Divergent Connectivity in Social-Emotional Pathways" (that title never gets any simpler, does it?). It details the structural differences in the brains of people with SPD and those of people with an ASD. As you may remember, the team found that, in SPD-only brains, there's a greater disconnection in some areas of white matter when compared with ASD brains. This may mean that sensory processing is overall more difficult for people with SPD than with an ASD when it comes to the processing of sight, sound, and touch. The team also found that, in people with an ASD, the areas relating to the processing of facial emotion and language are different from neurotypical brains, but this isn't always the case in brains with SPD. This means that people with SPD do not necessarily feel challenged by reading and interpreting facial expressions of emotion or understanding and speaking words. Most importantly for understanding's sake, if you map SPD and ASD in the brain, much like Google Maps would map your route to work, the lines you'd draw across the brain to show the area that these differences span would differ based on whether the person has SPD only, an ASD only, or both an ASD and SPD. The "route" of SPD, ASD, and combined ASD-SPD are not the same.

The clearest differences between SPD and ASD can be seen in the DSM-5. Although SPD has yet to be included in this pivotal text, the symptoms of ASD are neatly outlined and can be useful for comparison.

In the DSM-5, the items below are the diagnostic criteria used by professionals to help identify and diagnose an ASD. Not all of the items need to be present for an ASD to be present (the items in the first section indicate a deficit across all fronts, although the second section requires two or more plus the entire first section, for example). I am simplifying the language to make it less clinical and more reader-friendly:

ASD

Social/Communication

    1a. Challenges related to the sharing of emotions, conversations, and interests

    1b. Reduced eye contact, body language and gestures, and facial expressions

    1c. Challenges in developing and maintaining relationships and friendships

AND

Behavior/Interests/Activities

2a. Repetitive movements (stimming), use of objects, or speech

2b. Inflexibility related to routines, ritualized patterns of behavior, desire for sameness

2c. Intensely focused, fixated interests on an object or subject

2d. Over- or under-responsivity to sensory information

Go back and re-read 2b and 2d. These two items of the ASD diagnostic criteria are the only ones that bleed into SPD. People with SPD struggle with the need for sameness related to sensory input because we're often over- or underwhelmed by sensory information, and so we tend to cling to routine to ensure our safety and processing abilities. I could make the case for 2a when it comes to the debate of whether or not people with SPD actually stim, but we're not known for repetitive parts of speech, like reciting a word over and over out loud, nor are we typically driven to use objects repetitively, like lining them up over and over.

We're also not known to typically struggle with social engagement, except when it comes to some delayed-diagnosis sensory adults. I say this because after decades of misunderstanding, frustration, and in some cases actual physical and emotional abuse, I know many SPD-only adults who cannot comfortably sustain platonic or romantic relationships. I think the key here is that they choose to refrain from social ties because of the pain they've experienced and continue to experience, and they are not just differently wired with respect to this function as in an ASD.

I hear some of you saying, *"Gee, Rachel, why do we have to go through all of the trouble to separate SPD and ASD? Why can't we just say that there's a wide spectrum of sensory issues out there, and perhaps SPD is at one end and ASD is at the other?"* While I clearly respect this view, I'm not entirely in agreement with this argument. Let me tell you why.

It's very important for those of us with just SPD to understand the differences between SPD and ASD because it helps to define the parameters of our condition as well as describe it better to others. Sensory issues were moved into the spotlight when autism began gaining attention in the 1990s and early 2000s, and so sensory issues are commonly thought of as one component of an ASD instead of a separate, distinct neurological condition that many people with an ASD also happen to have, as we're beginning to see it today. I deeply respect people with an ASD, but I don't personally have an ASD, so to say that I'm somewhere on the spectrum is untrue for me. I have SPD, which is a discrete condition worthy of being studied, written about, advocated for, and accepted by the medical community and our society at large so that others like me don't go undiagnosed for so long. Delineating what's SPD and what's ASD and seeing SPD as its own condition is crucial for those of us with SPD-only brains, as it validates our experiences and conveys to those in the world that what we have is also worthy of support and attention. Being intimately connected to ASD in concept is also supremely helpful for the cause, as—like a good, older cousin might do—ASD can take SPD by the hand, and the factions of the greater sensory community can support one another.

SPD—Difference? Disorder? Disability?

People have said to me, *"SPD isn't a disorder or a disability, it's a difference, and we need to embrace the entire spectrum of human differences out in the world."* I believe that SPD is a difference, a disorder, and a disability depending on the parameters of a situation and how I feel on a given day. On the days where my SPD makes me laugh—when I trip over our armchair and go flying across the living room—SPD is a *difference*. I know I'm unique and a bit of a klutz (understatement of the century), and I can see the humor in the situation. Sometimes, however, my patterns of thinking and behavior as they're set in the "typical" world make me feel *disordered*. I can't help but become my own cheering squad or firing squad, and I praise or berate myself liberally for the things I can and cannot do when compared to the average abilities of others. These are times when my SPD is a *disorder*. When I become entrenched in a particularly violent shutdown episode, when I can no longer process sight or sound and therefore cannot even walk myself home, my SPD is a *disability*. To say that SPD is merely a difference is to negate my rich and varied experiences of this condition and living in my unique body. Yes, there is a wide range of human experiences—if even just between ASD and SPD—and sure, ultimately we may be part of a larger spectrum of differences across the human experience, but to assimilate the words *disorder* and *disability* is to negate two crucial aspects of the condition.

The long and the short of SPD and ASD can be summed up like this:

1. SPD and ASD are different conditions with some common similarities

2. They impact different areas of the brain

3. Many people with an ASD also have SPD

4. Most people with SPD don't also have an ASD

5. People with SPD have the sensory and rigidity diagnostic items of an ASD but not the social and emotional items

6. People with SPD and ASD make up the greater community of people with "sensory issues"

Chapter 10
Putting It All Together

You now know everything that I know about sensory issues to date—from the basics of each sense to the ways in which SPD and ASD differ. I say "to date," because we're truly on the frontier of understanding right now. We're finally working in tandem across some pivotal fronts to make sense of SPD from every angle, and because we're in the process, who knows what novel tidbit we'll learn about sensory issues tomorrow and the next day? That's the most amazing thing about being a pioneering force in any given area—there's so much more to be discovered, so much more to teach people, so much more to learn. Making sense of sensory issues is ultimately a process.

Since my own journey began in 2010, I've been collecting the information in this book as someone might collect antiques. My collection is always growing. I am always on the hunt for something new and exciting, or even something new to me that I can display on the mantel. This is how I felt when I first read about the biological underpinnings of SPD, and it's how I felt when I first learned the theory behind blue-tinted lenses. With each find, my world becomes broader, and the way that I understand my experiences and myself shifts.

Here are what I hope are the top 15 newest items in your sensory library after reading this book:

1. We are all sensory beings living in a sensory world
2. We have eight senses
3. Some of us have sensory issues
4. Sensory issues include SPD
5. SPD has three major categories with even further subtypes
6. Studies are showing that SPD has neurological origins
7. Areas of the brain are structured differently in people with SPD vs. without SPD
8. SPD is not a childhood disorder; it's a lifetime disorder

9. Neuroplasticity in childhood makes SPD easier to treat

10. SPD can mimic mental health issues

11. Secondary mental health issues can also accompany SPD

12. Occupational therapy, psychotherapy, physical therapy, and vision therapy all help with SPD

13. Tools (like fidgets) and techniques (like visualization) also help with SPD

14. SPD and ASD have similarities but are not the same thing

15. Many people with an ASD also have SPD, but few people with SPD have an ASD

My advocacy work will never stop. I dream of a time when SPD will be a familiar condition to medical professionals, mental health professionals, and laymen alike. It's a time when no sensory child will go undetected and undiagnosed. I am proud to lead a community of delayed-diagnosis sensory adults just like me, but I will be even prouder when our ranks thin down, and we're all elderly—relics of a bygone era before we knew enough about the brain and the senses to make enough of a difference. I will be the first one to bid the delayed-diagnosis sensory adult experience the fondest farewell, even though these experiences have been the context of my own life.

If you're still reading, then you and I can stroll out of this last chapter together like sensory outlaws into the sunset. Turn and face the expansive sky as nighttime drains the day. Slip on our tinted glasses or gaze hungrily at the setting sun and the blink of lights on the horizon. Cue the credits, even.

Reference List

Websites

Adults and Teens

Rachel's Website: www.rachel-schneider.com

Rachel's Blog, Coming to My Senses: www.comingtosenses.blogspot.com

The SPD Foundation: www.spdfoundation.net

Eating Off Plastic: www.eatingoffplastic.wordpress.com

SPD Life: www.spdlife.org

Children and Parents

The SPD Foundation (see above)

The Sensory Spectrum: www.thesensoryspectrum.com

SPD Parent Zone: www.spdparentzone.org

Books

Adults and Teens

Heller, Sharon (2003). *Too Loud, Too Bright, Too Fast, Too Tight: What to Do if You Are Sensory Defensive in an Overstimulating World.* Harper Perennial.

Heller, Sharon (2013). *Uptight & Off Center: How Sensory Processing Disorder Throws Adults Off Balance & How to Create Stability.* Symmetry.

Kranowitz, C.S. (2016). *The Out-of-Sync Child Grows Up: Coping with Sensory Processing Disorder in the Adolescent and Young Adult Years.* New York: Perigee.

Children and Parents

Biel, Lindsay (2009). *Raising a Sensory Smart Child: The Definitive Handbook for Helping Your Child with Sensory Processing Issues.* Penguin Books.

Kranowitz, C.S. (1998). *The Out-of-Sync Child.* Perigee Books.

Laird, Chynna (2009). *Not Just Spirited: A Mom's Sensational Journey with Sensory Processing Disorder (SPD).* Loving Healing Press.

Miller, Lucy Jane (2014). *Sensational Kids: Hope and Help for Children with Sensory Processing Disorder.* Perigee Books.

O'Sullivan, Noreen (2014). *I'll Tell You Why I Can't Wear Those Clothes! Talking About Tactile Defensiveness.* Jessica Kingsley Publishers.

Veenendall, Jennifer (2009). *Why Does Izzy Cover Her Ears?* Autism Asperger Publishing Company.

Voss, Angie (2011). *Understanding Your Child's Sensory Signals: A Practical Daily Use Handbook for Parents and Teachers.* CreateSpace Independent Publishing Platform.

Articles

Kranowitz, Carol Stock (Winter 2013). The Out-of-Sync Child Grows Up. *Sensory Focus* Magazine.

Schneider, Rachel S.

(Spring 2014). An Ode to My Handler. *Sensory Focus* Magazine.

(Winter 2014). A Letter to Myself Many Years in the Making. *Sensory Focus* Magazine.

(December 2014). The Neurotypicals' Guide to Adults with Sensory Processing Disorder. *The Body is Not an Apology*.

(January 2015). What Everyone Should Know About Sensory Processing Disorder. *Mind Body Green*.

(Spring 2015). Reflections on the Sensory Self. *Sensory Focus* Magazine.

Tools

Weighted Blankets

The Magic Blanket, www.themagicblanket.net (Keith Zivalich)

Bibliography

Balm, James. (2014). The Subway of the Brain: Why White Matter Matters. Retrieved from http://blogs.biomedcentral.com/on-biology/2014/03/14/the-subway-of-the-brain-why-white-matter-matters/

Chang, Y.S., Owen, J.P., Desai, S.S., Hill, S.S., Arnett, A.B., Harris, J., ... Mukherjee, P. (2014). Autism and Sensory Processing Disorders: Shared White Matter Disruption in Sensory Pathways but Divergent Connectivity in Social-Emotional Pathways. *PLOS ONE.* http://journals.plos.org/plosone/article?id=10.1371/journal.pone.0103038

Changizi, Mark. (2009). Why Does Music Make Us Feel? *Scientific American.* Retrieved from www.scientificamerican.com/article/why-does-music-make-us-fe/

Davies, P.L. & Gavin, W.J. (2007). Validating the Diagnosis of Sensory Processing Disorders Using EEG Technology. *The American Journal of Occupational Therapy,* 61 (2), 176-189.

Nelson, C.A., Fox, N.A., & Zeanah, C.H. (2014). *Romania's Abandoned Children: Deprivation, Brain Development, and the Struggle for Recovery.* Massachusetts: Harvard University Press.

Owen, J.P, Marco, E.J., Desai, S., Fourie, E., Harris, J., Hill, S.S., ... Mukherjee, P. (2013). Abnormal White Matter Microstructure in Children with Sensory Processing Disorders. *Neuroimage: Clinical,* 2, 844-853.

Pappas, Stephanie. (2012). Early Neglect Alters Kids' Brains. Retrieved from www.livescience.com/21778-early-neglect-alters-kids-brains.html

Schaaf, R.C., Benevides, T., Blanche, E.I., Brett-Green, B.A., Burke, J.P., Cohn, E.S., ... Schoen, S.A. (2010). Parasympathetic Functions in Children with Sensory Processing Disorder. *Frontiers in Integrative Neuroscience*, 4, 1-11.

Glossary

Activities of Daily Living (ADLs)

Basic tasks of everyday life, like eating and getting dressed.

Anxiety Disorders

A family of chronic psychological disorders related to ongoing, intense, and overwhelming worry and fear. Anxiety disorders include Panic Disorder, Generalized Anxiety Disorder (GAD), Social Anxiety Disorder, and phobias.

Asperger's Syndrome

An Autism Spectrum Disorder (ASD) that is commonly thought to be on the high-functioning end of the spectrum. People with Asperger's often have challenges with social interaction, a restricted range of interests, and repetitive movements, although they typically don't experience any of the language delays prevalent in autism. Some also have sensory issues as well.

Attention-Deficit/Hyperactivity Disorder (ADHD)

A neurological condition that impacts a person's ability to pay attention to tasks and control their behavior.

Autism Spectrum Disorder (ASD)

A family of neurological conditions that are characterized by difficulties with verbal and nonverbal communication, social interaction, repetitive behaviors, and sensory sensitivities.

Autonomic Nervous System

The part of the nervous system that regulates our internal organs and related processes like breathing, heartbeat, and digestion.

Bipolar Disorders

A family of psychological disorders characterized by periods of severe depression and mania.

Cognitive Behavioral Therapy (CBT)

A type of time-limited and skill-based psychotherapy that focuses on solving problems in the present.

Cognitive Reframing

A psychological technique that helps us change the meaning we assign to an event.

Craving

The act of actively looking for and desiring a particular type of sensory input. Sometimes called "seeking."

Delayed-Diagnosis Sensory Adults

People with sensory issues who made it into adulthood before receiving a sensory diagnosis and related treatment.

Depersonalization

A state of being in which a person's own thoughts and feelings seem unreal.

Depressive Disorders

A family of psychological disorders characterized by depressed mood, diminished interest in pleasure, fatigue, weight issues, sleep issues, concentration issues, feelings of worthlessness, and thoughts of death.

Derealization

A state of being in which a person's surroundings seem unreal.

Diagnostic and Statistical Manual of Mental Disorders (DSM)

The American Psychiatric Association's main guidebook to identify and diagnose psychological conditions, as well as some neurological conditions.

Dissociative Disorders

A family of psychological disorders that relate to the impairment of one's normal state of awareness (about the self, others, and the environment) and impact one's sense of identity, memory, and consciousness.

Dyspraxia

A condition that impacts motor coordination.

Dysregulation

The temporary state of someone with sensory issues when they're unable to self-regulate and maintain a calm, poised, ready state. It's what happens when too much or too little sensory input is taken in by the differently wired system.

Eating Disorders

A family of psychological disorders that relate to abnormal eating habits.

Egocentrism

A type of thinking in Piaget's Stages of Cognitive Development in which a child can't see anyone else's perspective but their own.

Electroencephalogram (EEG)

A test that detects electrical activity in the brain.

Fidgets

Small tactile items that help people with sensory issues to focus.

Filling Your Sensory Bank

A technique to help someone with proprioceptive issues reconnect to their body and the space around them.

Generalized Anxiety Disorder (GAD)

An anxiety disorder characterized by chronic anxiety and worry about everyday life events.

Grey Matter

The areas of the brain with cell bodies.

Habituation

The process of getting used to a stimulus, like a light or a sound, by seeing or hearing it over and over again.

Handler

A partner, parent, or friend who helps someone with SPD operate in the sensory world by assisting them with their particular sensory challenges.

Hit the Deck

A full-bodied prone or supine recline on the floor that helps someone with proprioceptive issues reconnect to her or his body and feel calm.

Homeostasis

The tendency of the body to seek and keep internal balance.

Interoception

The sense related to the state of our internal organs.

Meltdown

A common reaction to too much sensory information. Characterized by intense anger and tears.

Neural Pathways

The brain's connecting nerve cells.

Neuroimaging

A specialty in charge of producing images of the brain.

Neurological

Relating to the brain, spinal cord, and/or nerves.

Neuroplasticity

The brain's ability to create new connections.

Neurotypical

Someone with typical neurology and without a neurological condition like SPD or an ASD.

Occupational Therapy

A form of therapy that helps people living with various physical, mental, and neurological conditions develop, improve, and restore independence in a very hands-on and practical manner.

Over-Responsive

A subtype of Sensory Modulation Disorder in which information from one or more of the senses is perceived as being especially intense and overwhelming.

Panic Disorder

An anxiety disorder characterized by panic attacks, or intense physical episodes of fear that feel like one is having a heart attack or dying.

Parasympathetic Nervous System

A branch of the Autonomic Nervous System that regulates digestion and sexual arousal as well as slows down the heart rate and lowers blood pressure. Studies show that people with sensory issues have lower parasympathetic activity than those without sensory issues.

Perception

The process of interpreting and processing the information taken in by the sense organs.

Personality Disorders

A family of psychological disorders that are characterized by maladaptive and rigid patterns of thoughts and behaviors that become an intrinsic part of the person and the personality.

Post-Traumatic Stress Disorder (PTSD)

A psychological disorder that follows experiencing or witnessing a particularly terrifying, tragic, or traumatic event.

Proprioception

The sense of where the body is located in physical space.

Proprioceptors

Cells located in our muscles, joints, and inner ear that provide information about the position of our limbs in space.

Psychotherapy

A type of therapy that uses scientifically validated procedures to help a person develop healthier ways of thinking, feeling, behaving, and engaging with themselves and the world around them.

Physical Therapy

A type of therapy related to rehabilitative health that uses exercises and equipment to help people regain and improve physical abilities.

Rational Emotive Behavior Therapy (REBT)

A type of psychotherapy that is action-oriented and helps teach people to identify, challenge, and replace self-defeating beliefs and thoughts with ones that promote well-being and goal achievement.

Regulation

Adjusting the level of alertness based on time of day and related sensory stimuli by either calming down or ramping up one's energy. People with sensory issues often struggle with regulation, and many are dysregulated.

Seasonal Affective Disorder (SAD)

A depressive psychological condition related to a particular season.

Sensation

The physical act of the sense organs being stimulated by the environment.

Sensory-Based Motor Disorder

A major subtype of Sensory Processing Disorder, including Postural Disorder and Dyspraxia, in which a person struggles with body position, movement patterns, and/or planning and executing complex movements.

Sensory Discrimination Disorder

A major subtype of Sensory Processing Disorder in which a person struggles with the perception of subtle qualities of people, places, and objects, like size and direction.

Sensory Hangover

The result of too much sensory input and too much energy used for the processing of this input. Typically happens the day following intense sensory processing and is characterized by exhaustion, hyper-sensitivity, and difficulty processing further sensory information.

Sensory Input

Input from the senses such as sight, sound, touch, or movement.

Sensory Integration Dysfunction

The former name for Sensory Processing Disorder.

Sensory Integrative Approach

An occupational therapeutic approach to treating sensory issues.

Sensory Issues

Differences in the processing of sensory information that can be challenging and sometimes problematic for the individual's well-being and functioning. Typically applies to both SPD and ASD.

Sensory Lifestyle

Sometimes called a "sensory program," "sensory buffet," or "sensory diet," a set of exercises, tools, and techniques that help a person remain focused and organized (regulated) throughout the day.

Sensory Overload

When the brain is so overwhelmed with sensory input from one or more of the senses that it cannot properly process the information. Most common among people with sensory issues and may lead to a meltdown or shutdown without the right kind of therapeutic intervention. Can happen to people without sensory issues as well.

Sensory Modulation Disorder (SMD)

A major subtype of Sensory Processing Disorder in which a person struggles with regulating their responses to sensory stimuli. SMD includes the Over-Responsive, Under-Responsive, and Craving subtypes.

Sensory Processing Disorder (SPD)

A neurological condition in which a person does not perceive or respond to sensory information in a typical fashion.

Shutdown

A common reaction to too much sensory information. Characterized by dissociation and fear.

Spectrum

The familiar name given to the autism spectrum or the range of conditions that falls under the autism umbrella.

Stimming

A form of self-regulation that helps a person with an ASD cope with anxiety, fear, anger, and intense sensory input. It's unclear whether or not traditional SPD regulating behaviors fall under this title.

Thought Stopping

The psychological technique of interrupting recurring, cyclical patterns of thought.

Transition

Moving from one activity, person, or environment to another. A particular challenge for people with sensory issues, because the next sensory experience cannot be gauged as easily and may be different, requiring extra processing effort.

Under-Responsive

A subtype of Sensory Modulation Disorder in which the individual is unaware of sensory information from one or more of the senses.

Vestibular

The sense related to balance, orientation, and our physical position relative to gravity. Balance.

Vineland Adaptive Behavior Scales II

A measure of adaptive behavior from birth through adulthood.

Vision Therapy

A type of therapy that uses a sequence of neurosensory and neuromuscular activities to strengthen visual skills and visual processing.

Visual Acuity

The clarity of vision.

Visualization

A cognitive tool used by psychotherapists to bring about a state of relaxation through the imagination.

Weighted Blanket

A blanket filled with poly pellets that provides calming proprioceptive input. The weight of a weighted blanket should always be 10% of a person's body weight plus one pound.

Weighted Lap Pad

A mini weighted blanket that goes across the lap. Useful for calming proprioceptive input during travel and while out in public.

Wilbarger Deep Pressure Brush

A deep pressure brush used as part of the Wilbarger Deep Pressure and Proprioceptive Technique.

Wilbarger Deep Pressure and Proprioceptive Technique

A technique developed by an occupational therapist and clinical psychologist that uses deep pressure and proprioceptive input to help people with various forms of SPD to regulate.

White Matter

The connecting areas of the brain.

Yoga Nidra

A conscious sleep-like meditation exercise that promotes calm and peace.

Acknowledgments

This book could not have come to fruition without the love and support of Jennifer Gilpin Yacio and the wonderful people at Sensory World. You've made my dream come true, and "thank you" does not even begin to do my appreciation justice.

I am beyond grateful to Sharon Heller for her willingness to write my foreword and for the impact her work has had on the sensory community. Thanks for your friendship, encouragement, and positivity.

Carol Kranowitz, you are one of the best things that have ever happened to my sensory life! I can't imagine getting this far without your unyielding belief in me, and I am beyond thankful to have you as a member of my sensory family.

Kellasaurus, aka Stedmayle, what can I say? You are my little sensory sister. Your levity and ability to laugh at all of the "crapsauce" stuff that SPD life throws your way is an inspiration, and your artwork is perhaps my favorite thing *evarrr*. Thank you for dressing up this guide with your drawings. This is like writing a note in your yearbook. 2 good 2 B anything but sensory. Borpo lurves yerr.

My book team mentors, Jonathan Alpert, Elizabeth David-Dembrowsky, and David Hahn—I swear I'll write that memoir next! Thanks for having patience with me and wanting to see my words in print as much as I did.

Elysa Marco, you are both my friend and my hero. The work that you do with your team continues to change my life and the lives of those like me with SPD every single day. I am eternally at your disposal and cannot wait to see what else you can teach us in the future.

Victor DelBene, thank you for being so patient and so willing to break down those beautiful and complex neurological studies and help me understand them. So many people will now understand crucial research studies because of your support.

Thanks to the sweet and smart Chloe Rothschild for consulting with me on text issues related to ASD. I am so impressed and proud of the work you do for the ASD community, and I'm honored to be advocating alongside you in our general sensory community. We truly are like sorbet and ice cream: delicious!

Thanks to the hilarious and wise Jennifer McIlwee Myers for consulting with me on issues related to Asperger's syndrome. Your vivid and frank emails always make me smile while giving me so much to think about.

Jennifer Hughes and Kelly Jurecko, you lovely sensory mamas, I am honored to be counted among your friends, and I am thankful for your support, encouragement, and partnership as we advocate as a complete community.

Thanks to Dr. Lucy Jane Miller, Susanne Geiler, and the entire SPD Foundation for supporting my advocacy efforts. Lucy, your passion for SPD is infectious, and Susanne, your emails always make me smile. I am so glad to know you both.

Rachel Cohen-Rottenberg, *The Neurotypicals' Guide* is what enabled me to write this book, and you are the reason it has gotten so much web-love. I can't thank you enough for taking a chance on me (but really, with our first names and our backgrounds, how could we go wrong?!).

I absolutely adore my friends in the greater SPD community! Viki, Terry, Jennie, Bob, Lecia, Nat and Caitlin, Mary, Jesse, Annetta, Sonia, Mary Beth, Beverly, Erica, Anna, Abby ... the list could go on and on—you guys are truly the greatest, and I am honored to know you and your stories.

Dan Travis, you get called out twice. You will always be my first sensory friend and mentor, and I am so thankful that you exist.

To my Coming to My Senses readers and followers, there'd be no me without you. Thank you for thinking this particular gal had something worthy to teach you about adult life with SPD. I am humbled by your support and enthusiasm for my writing and my perspective.

Jan Weiner, you are the singular reason that I am here and functioning so well today. You pointed out the sensory to me, even though it'd been right under my nose my entire life. Your simple understanding and acceptance of me as a person with this condition has completely changed my approach to my world and myself. Thank you for your tireless work. You have the power to effect such amazing change (for an example, look at me).

Abbey Brod Rosen and Jennifer Kelly, your work has made it possible for me to move through this world with the richest arsenal of tools and exercises. Thank you for making me feel more comfortable in my own skin.

Professors of the Ferkauf Graduate School of Psychology—especially the sweet sage who hooded me and mentored me, Dr. Gary McClain—and my grad school friends, thank you for welcoming the girl with the weird, blue aviators into your classrooms and lives, and for making me feel capable of anything.

BBdear, Banana, Bobo, Friendy, Krissy, Xal, Keytone, Peens, Lil' Bro, DCITP Girls, Amabel, Specmamacita, Mins, Team Cupcake, and Ashlee, I am the luckiest friend in the entire world. And speaking of friends, thanks especially to the Galsts, Mindlins, Franks, and Badings for embracing this quirky gal at every phase of life. Always love.

John, Derina, and Nancy, thank you for making me feel like such a valuable part of your work family.

To the extended Greenberg, Goodman, Schneider, and Becker families, thank you for honoring my challenges and for celebrating my strengths. Love especially to my Uncle Marty for the "keppie kisses"; to my cousin Lauren for always rescuing me; and to my beloved Great Aunt Shirley, who was like a grandma to me and asked all about this book before she passed away last spring.

To the extended Erich and Simon families, thanks for always reminding me to laugh. And especially to Michelle and Peter, thanks for creating such a loving, supportive, caring, and understanding man for me to marry.

Wonz, you little shmuddin' pop, you were my first partner in crime, and you continue to be one of my favorite people on this planet. Thanks for bringing the wonderful Billy into our lives. The four of us "kids" are one of the best things about being a part of our family. Sunshine on my shoulder ... you know the rest.

Papa, you were my first handler, and I still feel the safest when I know you're nearby. Thank you for making me in your spitting image, both in face and in disposition, and for cracking me up on a daily basis.

Mom, you are my best friend. You get me, you champion me, you kick me in the butt, you struggle with me, you cry with me, you laugh with me, and you remind me that, after all of it, this world is really a beautiful place. I couldn't do it without you.

Sparky, it's simple, really, like love should be. You are my other half. You make me laugh, you keep me safe, and you remind me of my strength. The world can be a complex place for people with SPD, but my sensory life feels so much easier with you by my side. Thank you for making my days so bright. I love you.

About the Author

Rachel S. Schneider, M.A., MHC, is a writer, mental health counselor, de-layed-diagnosis SPD adult, and leader of the adult SPD community. She is the author of the popular sensory blog, *Coming to My Senses*, and the hit articles "The Neurotypicals' Guide to Adults with Sensory Processing Disorder" and "What Everyone Should Know About Sensory Processing Disorder." Rachel lives in New York City with her husband and handler, Joshua Erich.